Motherhood and Autism

Motherhood and Autism

*An Embodied Theology of
Mothering and Disability*

Eilidh Campbell

WIPF & STOCK · Eugene, Oregon

Wipf and Stock Publishers
199 W 8th Ave, Suite 3
Eugene, OR 97401

Motherhood and Autism
An Embodied Theology of Motherhood and Disability
By Campbell, Eilidh
Copyright © 2021 Hymns Ancient & Modern - SCM Press
All rights reserved.
Softcover ISBN-13: 978-1-6667-5127-7
Hardcover ISBN-13: 978-1-6667-5128-4
Publication date 6/17/2022
Previously published by SCM Press, 2021

Contents

Did he ever begin himself, though?
Mother, you made him small, it was you that began him;
he was new to you, you arched over those new eyes the
  friendly world, averting the one that was strange.
Where, oh where, are the years when you simply displaced
  for him,
with your slender figure, the surging abyss?
You hid so much from him then;
made the nightly-suspected room harmless,
and out of your heart full of refuge
mingled more human space with that of his nights.
Not in the darkness, no, but within your far nearer presence
you placed the light, and it shone as though out of friendship.
Nowhere a creak you could not explain with a smile, as
though you had long known when the floor would behave
itself thus ...
And he listened to you and was soothed ...

Rainer Maria Rilke (1921)
'Duino Elegies: The Third Elegy'

Acknowledgements

They say that 'it takes a village' to raise a child. I have learned that it also takes a village to write a book.

First, thank you to 'Naomi', 'Scarlet' and 'Abigail', the brave women who so generously offered to lend their voices to this research. Your stories have taught me, moved me and inspired me.

The research that contributed to this volume was supported by Trinity College Glasgow. I am grateful to them for providing me with the opportunity to undertake this research. Thank you to Dr Katie Cross for urging me to publish; without your encouragement, these pages would likely never have been read. Thanks must also be given to SCM Press, in particular David Shervington, for their belief and patience in this work.

The completion of the book would also not have been possible without the enduring patience, support and friendship of my doctoral supervisor Professor Heather Walton. It has been a long journey, but she has accompanied me with grace and kindness.

Thanks must also be given to others within the University of Glasgow TRS Department for their feedback and support. In particular to Dr Clare Radford, for her invaluable insight and solidarity, and to Doug Gay for his thoughtful perspective. Thanks also to Dr Patricia 'Iolana, for her inspiring tutelage as both a mother and a thinker.

Thank you also to the staff at Goldenhill School, in particular Hazel Campbell and Sharon Lappin, for nurturing the conditions in which Micah has been able to thrive.

Thanks also to the friends and family who have offered their support and belief in me throughout this process. Particularly to 'the Divers sisters' (Nicola, Caitlin, Rachel) for providing feedback on this research, and for their unfailing friendship over the years. Thanks to Rachael Kydd, Karen Kenny, Grant Black and the Prices for offering me respite from this journey, and for their cherished friendship to Micah. Thank you to Kenzie, for being my son without birth, and the yin to Micah's yang.

Thank you to the Anderson family: Colin, Ryan, Ben, and most of all, Carolyn. You have been mother to Micah when he has needed more than me. Without you, Micah would not have become the person he is.

Thank you to my sister, Mhairi, and my aunt, Catherine, for supporting us all during our worst days.

Thank you to my parents, for instilling in me a passion for learning and a pride in it. For my mother, whose absence I feel every day. You taught me to 'always leave others better than you find them', and your love, strength and kindness continue to inspire me to be better. For my father, who is and ever will be, Micah's best friend.

Thank you to my husband, Sam. I do not have the words to express my thanks for having you in our lives. Your love has made me the best version of myself, and I would not be who I am without you beside me.

Finally, thank you to my son, Micah, my warrior prophet. Your strength of character, creativity and resilience never ceases to amaze me. I have never been prouder of anything more in my life than the opportunity to be your mother.

Prologue: The Beginning

After a long and arduous pregnancy, I remember his first months seeming effortless. We existed in a blissful bubble. Placid but inquisitive, he fed well, slept well, laughed and cuddled. He was affectionate, but not needy. I was naively smug in my ability to mother this tiny human. We knew each other intuitively, him and I. Two halves of a whole. But as his first birthday neared ... our symbiosis began to fragment; dissolving slowly, but insidiously.

By eight months old, my once peaceful baby had become habitually disconsolate. His cries were impossible to predict and even more impossible to soothe. Something had shifted with him and me. Imperceptible, yet pivotal. A gnawing unease had begun to form in my belly. The intuitive ease with which I had always been able to antici-pate his needs had evaporated, seemingly overnight, and I was paralysed by my inability to understand him. Some-thing was wrong.

It felt like weeks since he had slept. Those days had turned into nights – nights in which daylight was simply replaced by the glow of the alarm clock, the minutes and hours ticking by almost mockingly. Those nights his cries, seemingly without purpose or interruption, would seem to last an eternity. I nursed. I held. I sang. I paced. One particular night marked the end of a week so long I could no longer do anything but sit on the bed and rock, trying futilely to guide my screaming child to a breast he did not want. By the time morning came, the soft light flickering through the curtains, I too was weeping. 'Please stop,' I murmured, over and over, a record scratched and jumping, constantly repeating; a desperate nursery rhyme that calmed neither him nor me.

My mother joyfully threw open the bedroom door, brandishing a huge balloon and a bouquet of flowers. 'It's Mother's Day!' she exclaimed. I had forgotten. Of course I had, the night had lasted weeks. The realization that I had welcomed my first Mother's Day broken and weeping, and that I had not been the one to first waken the wonderful creature before me with the flowers and excitement that she greeted me with, wrought fresh sobs from my chest. My mother's smile faltered as she took in the scene before her. Wordlessly, she took the baby from my arms. 'It's ... he's ... and I ... I can't,' I wheezed between sobs, staring down at the now empty space in my arms. With my baby deftly tucked under one arm, my mother turned her attention to her baby, now grown. Gently, she eased me back into bed.

'Oh, my darling,' she said. 'But you can. There will be many more Mother's Days, and many more nights like this before them. This baby will take every last ounce of energy and love you have, and you will still find more to give him. That's what it means to be a mother. And that's why we get the flowers.' As always, my wonderful mother was right. There would be many more Mother's Days. There would be many more flowers. But there would also be many more tears.

Introduction

A few tentative weeks after my son was born, I took him to my mother's church so that she could proudly display him to her friends. Her minister, who had known us since I was the same tiny bundle wrapped in blankets, enquired as to his name. 'Micah,' I shared.

He laughed, deep and knowingly. '"The Warrior Prophet"', he said. 'Well, you've set yourself up for a challenge there.'[1] How right he was.

My son was diagnosed with autism when he was six. The years prior to this were filled with confusion, frustration, fear and guilt. My beautiful, sweet-natured child seemed to disappear without warning, leaving behind a furious, terrifying stranger, whose actions and motives were inexplicable even to him. While we have always travelled hand in hand, just him and me, the road has been far from smooth. Practical theologians John Swinton and Harriet Mowat suggest that 'the questions that emerge in the light of the human experience of God are often different from those which emerge from the solitude of the academic's office' (Swinton and Mowat, 2006, p. 7). This particular book has emerged from a period of both light and dark, from bewilderment and uncertainty, from anguish and joy.

It has now been six years since his diagnosis. While we have journeyed a long way from the dark and bewildering days of pre-diagnosis, that road has been paved with tumultuous, twisting and circuitous emotions. As a theologian, who became the mother of a child with autism, I attempted to locate my maternal experience within the theologies available to me.

Surely, I thought, I would find myself somewhere on the pages of such books? Surely, I would stumble across our pain, our joy, our fury or our triumph on a shelf somewhere, and be able to apply some meaning or understanding to our experience? Yet this was not to be the case.

Despite increasing research confirming that autism, peculiarly and significantly, has been found to impact maternal well-being and mental health more profoundly than other developmental conditions (Estes et al., 2009, p. 376; Giallo et al., 2011, p. 466; Zhang et al., 2015, p. 29), very little attention has been given to how autism affects mothers; what challenges autism presents in everyday life, how these challenges meaningfully and substantially change the lived experience of motherhood, and how this really feels for the women who are living it.

In the course of this journey, I was approached by a friend and educator who enquired whether I would be willing to facilitate what she, quite aptly, called a 'Meet and Greet' for other mothers of those children who had additional support needs.[2] In supporting these families, this wonderful woman saw that the network of support available to them was insufficient in terms of what they really needed. These women did not need to be taught more about autism, or how to parent their autistic child. Parents of children on the spectrum learn very quickly to be experts not only in autism but in their *own* spectrum children, becoming their advocates and champions (Nicholas et al., 2016, p. 926).

However, the emotional responses that can be seen to accompany the myriad of challenges faced in mothering a child with a lifelong developmental condition such as autism are often complicated and conflicting. The struggles of parents whose children are on the autism spectrum are thus often carefully and skilfully hidden. What my friend had identified, and what I myself had been becoming aware of, was that mothers had no space to speak of such challenges. They were silenced, often ashamed, in their struggle; caught between love for their children and utter exhaustion. To express grief or disappointment in our mothering situation can often feel like a denial of our child. There is a gnawing fear underlying such disclosures;

the fear that others may think we do not love our children enough if we admit to such emotions. The stigma associated with confessing such complicated feelings is profoundly prohibitive, and so the world of the mother of a child with autism can be a lonely, silent place.

In reflecting upon this silenced struggle, theirs and mine, I considered that perhaps one of the most challenging aspects of the parental experience of autism is that it is often hidden; it is marginalized socially, academically and theologically. This occlusion is perhaps in part a consequence of the fact that autism remains resistant to any singular perspective or 'discipline'; contention remains as to whether autism can be defined as a disability, as a psychological condition, or indeed as merely a point on the 'spectrum' of human neurodiversity. This book intends not to unravel this ambiguity, but rather to illuminate it, exploring the ways in which autism can be seen to be both shaped by, and yet resistant to, social and theological constructions of disability.

Situating the context: autism

Autism is a lifelong developmental condition currently impacting 1.041 per cent of the UK population (or the equivalent of 700,000 people).[3] It is characterized by delayed development in early childhood, and abnormalities in three specific areas of cognitive function: social interaction, communication and behaviour. However, while autism can be seen to exist as a distinct diagnostic category, its symptoms are so diverse and varied in both severity and complexity that it remains a much misunderstood condition. Its cause is unknown, and its full definition is still to be established. For this reason, discussions of autism often involve the disciplinary boundaries of mental health, disability, sociology and ethics.

I propose that it is precisely this ambiguity, and lack of understanding, in relation to autism that has led it to be an issue that is largely ignored theologically. Professor John Swinton critiques the lack of current research that examines how religion, complete with abstract concepts, metaphors and symbols, is interpreted and understood by individuals who 'think differently' – as is assumed to be the case with individuals with autism. If, as Swinton and Trevett consider, we are to uphold the premise that spirituality is a fundamental human right, then the seriousness of failing to adequately respond to the challenge of developing accessible theologies for individuals with autism becomes a pressing concern (Swinton and Trevett, 2009, p. 2).

Although still woefully few, theologies that focus on autism as a lived experience that is generative for theological thinking are beginning to emerge. Dominant models in disability theology tend to link autism with issues of accessibility and inclusion, to those of hospitality and acceptance. Approaching autism from a biblical perspective, writers such as William Stillman (2006) and Mathew and Pandian (2010) have suggested that the Church must be open to reinterpreting traditional Christian narratives from an autistic viewpoint, noting that the ways in which autistic individuals 'think differently' can in fact provide significant insight and revelatory potential in challenging our commonly accepted interpretations of the Bible. Howell asserts that, 'The task of the church is to create new metaphors to describe timeless principles and to recreate those metaphors when they become uncomfortable for us' (Howell, 2015, p. 152).

However, despite making strides in bringing autism into the theological conversation, such moves are not unproblematic. Grant Macaskill, himself a theologian and member of the Church, who is also on the autism spectrum, is sceptical of the value of efforts that seek to construct a 'biblical hermeneutics of autism' as a means of making the Church 'theologically accessible'. While he acknowledges that contributions such as the work of Mathew and Pandian (2010) are well-intentioned in promoting inclusivity, he suggests that they ignore the fact that the Bible existed many centuries before any conception of autism had been known about or considered, so any attempt to 'read autism' into the Bible is arguably an academic exercise with little value to current experiences of autism (Macaskill, 2019, p. 43). Such polarity on the theological 'spectrum' highlights the fact that autism is not only new to the theological conversation, but is also short of conversation partners.

Arguably the most significant dialogues to emerge draw strongly from theological models that propose that inclusivity requires genuine acceptance of difference, not merely interpretation or adaptation. Interestingly, the most prominent theological contributions from this perspective have come from theologians who are themselves fathers of children on the autism spectrum. John Gillibrand (2009), Tom Reynolds (2008) and Brian Brock (2019) have all drawn on their own experiences to look at the theological tension provoked by having a child with autism, challenging the Christian community to see their children through their eyes.

Whose knowledge? The problem with seeing and hearing

Examining an issue such as autism, in all its complexity and contradictions, is fraught with tensions and problems. In prefacing their accounts, both Brock and Reynolds stress the apprehension they felt in sharing not only their lives on the page, but those of their children. This anxiety, particularly within the context of disability, leads to a minefield of ethical and moral concerns. First and foremost, there is the question of authority, in terms of who has the right to speak on a subject that so intimately involves the life of another. This is particularly problematic in the context of disability, in which issues of capacity and consent are often murky. There is the inherent danger that in drawing on the lives of those assigned such a label, particularly when those lives are children's, that one might be seen to be exploiting the experiences of a vulnerable other to suit their own ends. Furthermore, there is the danger that in reflecting on a relationship with such an 'other', the subject themselves become a mere object of tragedy. Brian Brock cautions that:

In practice, virtually every mother or couple faced with a diagnosis of a genetic abnormality draws on anecdotal experiences and accounts of the lives of the disabled and their care givers ... one of the dominant tropes for such stories presents them as tragic works of compassion by devoted parents (usually mothers, ground down by the burden of caring for the very children whose own stories disappear within the 'tragedy' that their lives are presumed to embody). (Brock, 2019, p. 81)

Brock here highlights the dangers of parents (mothers, it would seem, particularly) presenting their children as a 'burden' to carry, negating their own ability to tell their stories, and indeed their own value as individuals. The act of sharing narratives, particularly when they involve the life of another, is one that requires a critical and thoughtful theological response. Clare Wolfteich observes that:

If listening to narratives is to become 'an act of resistance' or an act of community and solidarity, practical theologians must do the difficult work of reflecting theologically upon others' narratives without co-opting them, without writing over them, sanitizing and homogenizing them. (Wolfteich, 2017, p. 133)

How much to share, and to what extent the sharing will cause potential hurt or embarrassment to my child and our wider family, is a deep concern for me. My son is 12 now, but articulate beyond his years. I am aware that he could, and very well may, read this in the not so distant future. While writing this book, he has often sat beside me. He will at times peer over my shoulder as I type or ask me what I am working on. It has been important to me to be honest with him about what I am writing, and why. I have been fortunate, though, that he has a remarkably pragmatic understanding of the challenges his attempts to navigate his autism has created for others, particularly myself. I have had to continually weigh the potential benefit of the information I am choosing to share against its potential harm to myself and my family.

Some of the challenges that I have chosen to write about were so all-consuming, so exhausting and overwhelming, both emotionally and physically, that there have been points in this process when they have simply been too raw and too painful to write about. Some of this book, consequently, has been written back to front, or from the middle out, during times when the more emotionally charged issues were simply too difficult to write about. I therefore urge readers to utilize the same self-care in reading the book. The issues are particularly sensitive – issues that may provoke strong and unsettling emotions. In shining a spotlight on such issues, I am not intending to be deliberately provocative, or to provide mere decorative flourish. In light of such possible criticisms, I am at pains to stress that the book does not approach the issue of autism from the perspective that it is a tragedy, neither for individuals with autism nor for the people who care about them. Rather, it is an honest admission that autism presents challenges that make life undeniably difficult for those who live alongside them.

While current and emerging theological reflections are beginning to shed light on this complex and conflicting lived experience, I found that my own lived experience remained persistently absent from the texts I so urgently explored. The harder I sought, the more 'missing' I seemed to be. In attempting to 'read' my life in between the lines of others' experiences, I often found that I had to interpret what were, admittedly, familiar experiences, but through an unfamiliar (and exclusively) male, Christian perspective. I found myself at once both inside, and yet outside, of the 'theological conversation'.

While I am a practical theologian, schooled within a predominantly Christian setting, I think it is important to be clear that I am writing 'outside' of the Christian context in which current theologies of disability predominantly – and theologies of autism particularly – situate themselves. I do not belong to any particular faith tradition and it is arguably this lack of belonging that compelled me to study theology in the first place. However, this 'outsider status' has been challenging as a practical theologian, in many different, complex and insidious ways. It is often assumed that I will present my reflection through the lenses above, which – for many reasons – is problematic.

Therefore, I will not attempt to offer a biblical interpretation of the meanings and potentialities of autism, nor stress the Christian imperative to 'love thy neighbour'. First, because this approach has already been offered, and in a much more nuanced and sincere way than I could replicate. Furthermore, to do so would be disingenuous, in feigning to belong to a community that I do not belong to. Instead, the book offers an interdisciplinary perspective, drawing from literature on autism, disability and motherhood, both within and outside the context of practical theology. This may lead to some readers questioning whether this work is indeed theological at all. In response, I propose that this question highlights a more pressing concern in the way we construct knowledge, an issue I will return to in the concluding sections of the book.

Maternal knowledge: the turn to lived experience

Although Brian Brock and Tom Reynolds deal wonderfully with the issue of being the father of a child on the autism spectrum, and while many of these experiences resonated deeply with my own, I could not shake off the question – but where are the mothers? Perhaps it is assumed that parenting affects mothers and fathers 'the same'; however, as I will go on to argue, the daily realities of mothers and fathers raising any children are often starkly different. In respect to autism, I will go on to show that mothers are distinctly, and peculiarly, affected by their relationship to autism in a myriad of complex and interrelating ways. Such complexity requires a deeper theological reflection not only on autism itself, but on the ways in which theology looks at issues of motherhood.

As a feminist practical theologian, mother to a child with autism, and friend to other women who share this lived experience, I am not only deeply implicated within the subject I am researching, but live and embody the experiences about which I am writing. I am not a neutral observer of an objective reality; rather, I am critically engaged in the process of researching my own experiences and their meanings through interpretive communication with others. While the potential for bias from such an 'insider position' has been treated with methodological unease (Anderson, 2006, p. 387; Sotirin, 2010, p. 5), it is my conviction that my embeddedness within this subject instead offers the potential for a rich and authentic production of knowledge. Describing this process as 'situated knowledge', Donna Haraway asserts that our epistemic location inevitably influences our epistemic making (Haraway, 1988, p. 581).

Heather Walton cautions that while life stories are an incredibly rich and generative source, 'life narratives are unwieldy and difficult to tame to our own ends' (Walton, 2014b, p. 14). Problematizing the use of biography as data, Wolfteich reminds us that in life writing, like any other form of writing, editorial decisions have to be made in which an author 'both reveals and conceals' what they wish others to know (Wolfteich, 2017, p. 22). In this sense, what the author chooses to leave out is often as revelatory as what they leave in. In an attempt to bridge the silences that I may (intentionally or inadvertently) create, I have chosen to augment my own reflections by turning to the voices of other mothers with children on the spectrum.

The book is therefore a reciprocal process. Undertaking interviews with three women with children of differing genders and ages within my own local context, I have sought to question the gaps and silences of the literature through hearing the stories of others. These three mothers have volunteered to share their unique experiences of the challenges and complexities of mothering a child on the spectrum, and give insights into an aspect of mothering that remains all too invisible. While I had entered into our dialogue armed with questions, I found that we had little need of them once we began to talk. The desire to break the silence that they had experienced was palpable.

Their experiences and their stories flowed freely once given the space to do so, and although we are each very different women with very different lives, so many of our experiences echoed with each other, affirming my observation that despite the multitude of characteristics associated with autism, there are many characteristics of the mothering experience that are shared across temporal, social and cultural contexts. As Isasi-Díaz asserts, the process of collating different voices and allowing different perspectives to shine through allows an organic and authentic revealing of connections, 'creating a tapestry in which one can see the similarity of experiences much more than dissimilar experiences' (Isasi-Díaz, 2004, p. 142).

American practical theologian Mary Moschella, considering the therapeutic potential of sharing life narratives, observes that 'the opportunity to speak out loud, hearing one's own voice and being asked for one's own judgement, is an empowering experience' (Moschella, 2016, p. 373). It soon became clear that choosing to take part in this process was not merely an altruistic gesture by these women to assist me in my research, but rather an active and liberatory process of engagement with issues that strongly shaped their lived experiences in ways they had previously been unable to share.

Motherhood is hard. What is harder still is that we are often left unable to speak of how hard it can be without fear of shame or judgement. As a consequence, the real, lived experience of motherhood can become hidden, stigmatized and silenced. The feelings, experiences and stories we hold inside can become lost as we are unable to find a meaningful space in the narrative of motherhood that allows for them to be told. Joan Laird describes this as the 'unstory': the stories that are too shameful or painful for us to share (Laird, 1991, p. 437). It is this aspect of motherhood, the 'unstories', which we feel compelled to keep hidden, that is too often neglected in our reading of maternal experience.

In situations such as these, Heather Walton observes that 'there may be times when we take brave decisions to share experiences that are painful to us, because their telling may be of benefit to others' (Walton, 2014b, p. xxix). I have made the decision in the book that the potential benefit to others in sharing our stories will outweigh the potential harm in telling them; I have been encouraged by others who have made this same decision and chosen to share their lives on the page. By offering an honest, sometimes painful, retelling of these moments, I hope I have produced a meaningful and authentic engagement with an issue that is troublingly silent in current discussions. And so, brave or otherwise, in revealing and reflecting on our 'unstories', this book intends to highlight aspects of maternal experience that have hitherto been omitted from theological debates and to explore how such narratives may prove productive in provoking new ways of thinking theologically about hidden lived experiences.

Structure of the book

As I have highlighted, autism is a condition that traverses disciplinary boundaries. The experience of mothering in the context of autism, therefore, is similarly complex. For this reason, I have divided the book into three parts. Part 1 gives an overview of the historical, medical and cultural constructions of autism, examining how these can be seen to contribute to the complexity of autistic lived experience. Part 2 explores the relationship between autism and disability, further examining the issues raised in Part 1, through the lens of dominant sociological and theological discussions on disability. Part 3 looks to the experience of mothering, exploring how prevailing models of motherhood can be seen to be distinctly, and peculiarly, implicated in the history of autism. This section will explore how the complex symptoms of autism, institutional barriers to support, and problematic constructions of motherhood come together to create a distinct form of maternal struggle, experienced and resisted in everyday life. In concluding, I propose that the lived experience of the mothers explored in this book necessitates a theological response that attends to the complexity and unsettled nature of lived experiences that resist incorporation into the standard frameworks of knowledge. It requires a theology of 'unresolvement'.

Part 1: Autism, ambiguity and unusual beginnings

Chapters 1 and 2 trace the complex history of autism in its emergence as a recognizable, distinct condition. Chapters 3 and 4 explore the characteristics of autism, identifying the impact their complexity and ambiguity has in delaying diagnosis and support. Chapters 4 and 5 then turn to a discussion of how diagnosis is experienced by parents, exploring the fluctuating and often conflicting emotional journey that an autism diagnosis presents. Engaging with disability literature that presents diagnosis as a form of medical authority over disabled lives, Chapter 6 examines how the label of autism is received, experienced and, in some cases, resisted.

Part 2: Disability, normalcy and stigma

Chapters 7, 8 and 9 explore the construction of disability as a label of lived experience, examining how the competing categories of 'normalcy' and 'deviancy' have constructed dichotomous and polarized understandings of disability that provoke stigma in unique – and, sometimes, dangerous – ways. Chapter 10 draws on mothers' narratives to reveal how such stigma is experienced and resisted in everyday life. Chapters 11 and 12 examine disability as a social construct, exploring how such societal struggles are lived and experienced by mothers of children on the autism spectrum, and evaluating the usefulness of communitarian and liberation theologies of disability in attending to disability as a social issue.

Part 3: 'Every day is a struggle' – mothers 'en la lucha'

Chapter 13 examines the particularity of mothering a child on the autism spectrum, exploring how mothers have been uniquely implicated in the historical narrative of autism. Chapter 14 explores how these particularities come together to create distinct maternal experience of struggle that can be seen to be most significantly played out within the 'domestic' context of the 'everyday'. Engaging with feminist theologies relating to struggle, the everyday, and the generative potential of maternal thinking, Chapter 15 presents the more active/autonomous role of mothers in resisting both social and domestic sources of struggle.

Chapter 16 discusses the role of theodicy in maintaining problematic constructions of struggle and suffering in theological contexts, challenging the dominant theological imperative of reconciliation/overcoming.

In the Conclusion, I propose a theological turn that is more cognizant of the complex, ambiguous and unresolved 'messiness' of life as it is lived – a turn to 'pragmatic unresolvement'.

Notes

1 The name 'Micah' has its origins from the Hebrew 'Mikhayhu', meaning 'he who is like God'. The book of Micah in the Old Testament prophesies judgement on the kingdoms of Israel and Judah, and draws on themes of injustice, particularly towards the poor and the marginalized. It is considered one of the earliest, and most accurate, prophecies of Christ's birth, and concludes with a message of hope in salvation through God.

2 For the clarity of non-Scottish readers, 'greet' in this context refers to the practice of 'greetin'', a very Scottish way of describing sobbing one's heart out.

3 See http://researchbriefings.files.parliament.uk, accessed 13.04.20.

PART I

Autism, Ambiguity and Unusual Beginnings

I tried to remember a time before. It had not always been this way, had it? It was in his last year of nursery that it all began, wasn't it? ... Wasn't it? I tried to retrace our steps, all the while painting over the sleepless nights, the furious tantrums, with the rosy tint of denial. Yet those little moments stubbornly refused to be painted over and began to take on new vividness, new meanings, under my now critical gaze.

I remembered when he had just turned one, and suddenly refused to wear the red dungarees I so loved him in. Every time I buckled the straps, he furiously tore them off, standing indignantly in his nappy shaking his head. At the time, I found his stubbornness amusing. He knew what he liked. I took pride in what I perceived to be his maturing personality; he was choosing his style. Looking back now, it was the beginning of a slow, insidious and seemingly arbitrary rejection of anything he did not like the feel, colour or fit of. By the time he was two, he could tolerate only a handful of items of clothing; those that he would tolerate he could not bear to grow out of and would continue to wear even after they had long stopped fitting.

I remember one morning drinking coffee with his 'aunt', my childhood friend. She was my sister formed without blood, and she lived with us in his first few years. Micah was playing contentedly on the floor with his toy cars, lost in his own world. He was always content with his own company, rarely demanded attention for the sake of attention. She was watching him, but her gaze had an intentness beyond the pride of a loving aunt. She quietly observed as he pulled his cars out of the box and lined them carefully and studiously up by colour in a row. He would put them all back and then repeat the process again and again.

'He knows his colours,' I said brightly, if a little uncertainly. Something was wrong. She was unreachable in that moment. I could sense that something had shifted in her perception, but I didn't know what. 'He doesn't drive his cars,' she said softly. It was true. He didn't zoom his cars around the floor, simulating crashes or using the chairs as tunnels as her brother had done. The eldest of five siblings, she knew babies. Was he different from the babies she had nurtured before? We have never spoken about it. Looking back, I wondered if, in that moment, she knew. It was to be many years from that moment before any of us would have an answer.

I

Autism: An Enduring Enigma

Perhaps one of the most defining characteristics of the condition commonly known as autism is its difficulty to define. While there can be seen to be a series of shared characteristics, the ways in which these characteristics present in any given individual are unpredictable and varied (Burack et al., 2001, p. 11). Why one set of symptoms may be present in one individual with autism yet not with another is a mystery that we are no closer to solving. Dr Stephen Shore, a professor in special education and himself autistic, once famously declared, 'If you have met one person with autism ... you have met one person with autism.'[1] Having had the privilege and opportunity through both my son and my work to meet other children, and adults, on the autism spectrum, I can say this to be true. I have never met another Micah, nor have I met any individual with autism who I could say was just like another. They are all brilliantly, curiously, inexplicably different. This is perhaps one of the most simultaneously wonderful and problematic features of autism: that one could spend years charting the behaviours and peculiarities of one autistic individual, only to discover the findings have little to no relevance to another.

The inconsistency and unpredictability in the symptoms of autism could undoubtedly be seen as contributing to the decades of confusion, misrepresentation and conflicting theories surrounding autism as a diagnostic category. Despite first being documented as a distinct category of observable symptoms in the early 1940s, there continues to be debate as to whether autism can be seen to be a psychological, biomedical or environmental condition (Wing, 1996, p. 33; Loveland, 2001, p. 17). Furthermore, increased visibility and understanding of autism notwithstanding, there remain some who continue to question whether autism is, in fact, a 'real' condition at all.[2] The ambiguity in the causes, symptoms and presentation of autism has resulted in it being a condition that is notoriously difficult to diagnose, with no current uniformly agreed-upon methods of management or support.

The apparent 'spike' in autism diagnoses in the last century has given rise to a myriad of competing, conflicting and often controversial theories as to why such an acceleration has taken place, confounding much of the confusion that already existed regarding autism as a condition (Silberman, 2015, p. 6). In order to unravel some of this confusion, understanding how autism presents itself and how it came to emerge as a diagnostic category may shed considerable light as to why, decades into our collective awareness of autism, it continues to be such a misunderstood and misdiagnosed condition. In what follows, I will explore the development of autism as a contested condition, charting the historical turbulence and conflicting research agendas that have complicated autism research and, consequently, autistic experience.

Emergence of autism: a legacy of confusion

Kanner's Syndrome

> These characteristics form a unique 'syndrome,' not heretofore reported, which seem rare enough, yet is probably more frequent than is indicated by the paucity of observed cases ... To satisfy the need for some terminological identification of the condition, I have come to refer to it as 'early infantile autism.' (Kanner, 1943, p. 242)

In 1943, Dr Leo Kanner released his seminal article, 'Autistic Disturbances of Affective Contact', which would later form the blueprint of clinical understandings of autism for generations to come. De-camped from Germany during World War Two, Kanner had become a respected child psychologist working out of Johns Hopkins Memorial Hospital in Baltimore in the early 1940s when he began to receive children who were, at such point in time, considered 'lost causes'. Many had exhausted other diagnostic avenues, most had been declared schizophrenic, mentally retarded, psychopathic, even deaf and mute. Some of these children had confounded diagnosis, yet all shared a distinct commonality – their parents were desperate for answers to the enigmas that were their children. For such children, prognosis was often lifelong institutionalization, and so the significance of Kanner's diagnosis cannot be understated for these families. For some, he was quite literally their last chance of having some semblance of a 'normal' family life.

The children brought to Kanner for assessment were afflicted by a myriad of unusual and distressing symptoms. After observing 11 such children, Kanner was able to identify common characteristics among those referred to him that differed from the characteristics presently defined as childhood schizophrenia, with which many of his subjects had been previously diagnosed. At times, we can discern almost a poignancy to Kanner's observations of the children in his study. He describes one boy, Richard, in the following way:

> He did not communicate his wishes but went into a rage until his mother guessed and procured what he wanted. He had no contact with people, whom he definitely regarded as an interference when they talked to him or otherwise tried to gain his attention. The mother felt that she was no longer capable of handling him, and he was placed in a foster home near Annapolis with a foster woman who had shown a remarkable talent in dealing with difficult children. Recently, this woman heard him say clearly his first intelligible words. They were, 'Good night.' (Kanner, 1943, p. 226)

What was relatively unique about Kanner's approach to psychology in the United States at the time was his belief that family history, in particular family dynamics, were significant factors in the diagnostic process. In addition to patient observations, Kanner also documented what he perceived to be common factors in the parents who presented their children: 'There is one very interesting common denominator in the backgrounds of all of these children ... *they all come from highly intelligent families*' (Kanner, 1943, p. 248). While he proposed that his patients indicated that autism was an innate, developmental condition, one that was described as being present from birth in many of his patients, Kanner also cited the similarities presented by the parents themselves as exacerbating, or indeed inducing, their children's symptoms. He notes, 'One other fact stands out prominently. In the whole group, there are very few really warmhearted fathers or mothers' (Kanner, 1943, p. 250).

Kanner, however, faced criticism from his peers as to the reliability of charting the development of children from birth retroactively, particularly when relying on a clinically accurate timeline of development from parents (Silberman, 2015, p. 210). Furthermore, the uniqueness of his diagnosis was challenged, with others in the field suggesting it was almost indistinguishable from the popular diagnosis of early childhood schizophrenia. Kanner maintained, however, that these children did not appear to be afflicted or distressed by their reality, but rather it was others' reality that these children found perplexing.

The children who were observed by Kanner all presented, in varying forms, with the diagnostic criteria for atypical early development. The most prevalent atypicalities among the children were development of speech, response to external stimuli or affection and personal independence. As a consequence, some of the children had been diagnosed as deaf or mute, as it was perceived that their inability to vocalize, respond to commands or instruction, or express their needs was a consequence of their inability to hear and therefore engage with the world around them. Kanner, however, believed that the children's inability to respond was not related to their inability to recognize speech, but rather their inability to infer any meaning or significance from it that was relevant to them (Kanner, 1943, p. 225). He observed that, 'The children's relation to people is altogether different ... people, so long as they left the child alone, figured in about the same manner as did the desk, the bookshelf, or the filing cabinet' (p. 246).

This, coupled with the lack of speech development, severely inhibited the children's ability, or seeming desire, to communicate. He observed that in instances where speech had developed in his patients, their speech pattern was unusual. Some of his patients could recite complex poems, lists or historical facts; however, they could not initiate spontaneous discussion or respond appropriately to questions put to them. The children displayed a literalness in their understanding of language; they were unable to infer meaning from speech (Kanner, 1943, p. 244). In addition to repetitive patterns of speech, the children all shared repetitive behaviours or preoccupations with objects, often simply spinning their object of choice for many hours rather than engaging in creative or imaginative play. Repetition could also be seen to reinforce the children's concern with routine, with many unable to cope or function with any deviation from their perceived 'norm'. Although it would be years before Kanner's article would gain recognition among his peers, the detailed observations on his patients' unusual idiosyncrasies would in fact, as we have seen, go on to inform the diagnostic model utilized today.

Hans Asperger: parallel histories

One of the enduring curiosities relating to autism is that it was first 'discovered' almost concurrently, by two separate individuals who had never met, on opposite sides of the world. While Leo Kanner is widely credited to have first observed autism as a distinct condition, in a serendipitous turn of events Dr Hans Asperger, a leading paediatric psychiatrist in Vienna, also found himself immersed in a similar world of bewildering and beguiling children a year later, in 1944. Although Kanner's article had already been published, it initially received little professional acclaim, and so it is generally accepted that it would have been highly unlikely to have crossed Asperger's path prior to his own publication. It is interesting to note, though, that one of Asperger's primary diagnosticians, George Frankl, also worked under Leo Kanner as a psychiatric paediatrician after fleeing Vienna in 1937 and, despite failing to be credited by Kanner, arguably contributed much to his research (Silberman, 2015, p. 180).

Asperger's patients similarly presented with delayed development and an extreme detachment from the social world. The children, like Kanner's, were preoccupied with objects or routines but seemed to have little or no interest in pleasing or bonding with their caregivers, to the extent that they were also often peculiarly violent towards others and seemingly without remorse (Asperger, 1944, translated in Frith, 1991, p. 77). Both men, however, had distinctly different approaches to their practice. Rather than rely on retrospective accounts of their condition, or subject these children to standardized tests (many of which they had already failed to measure on), Asperger and his colleagues at the Vienna clinic instead attempted to observe the children in as natural and comfortable an environment as they could create for them within a hospital setting, and instead painstakingly documented the minutiae of idiosyncrasies that formed each individual child as they naturally presented themselves (Frith, 1991, p. 7).

Modelled on Erwin Lazaar's compassionate therapeutic approach, the Vienna clinic was unparalleled at the time in its unique and innovative approach to therapy. Rather than adopting a purely medical model of intervention, the clinic combined biomedical treatment with education and play therapy in an 'intuitive synthesis' that accepted, rather than condemned, the children's differences (Frith, 1991, p. 7). The children were allowed to indulge in their respective proclivities, with Asperger and his team seemingly intuiting that allowing such obsessions to be explored could potentially break down some of the barriers that adults typically had in engaging with these children. As perhaps one of the earliest examples of person-centred and inclusive learning that we are only now, in very recent years, showing a shift towards in education, Asperger believed that it was the environment in which the children were forced to learn that was flawed, and not the children themselves.

One of the most marked differences between Kanner's and Asperger's syndromes, and that still distinguishes them today in the ICD-10 criteria, is Asperger's association of autistic traits and intelligence.[3] Asperger, like Kanner, had observed similar traits in both his patients and their parents and had also documented that the children came from unusually intelligent families. However, where Kanner saw the children as a product of an 'un-nurturing' environment, Asperger saw a potential biological link, raising the possibility that autistic 'intelligence' could be genetic in nature.

While the children on Asperger's ward were unable, or unwilling, to produce such knowledge in clinical tests, the environmental observations of the Vienna clinic proved invaluable in identifying that the children did, in the right setting, show a nuanced understanding and acumen on specific subjects. Asperger noted that despite some children being unable to engage in general communication or behaviour appropriately in social situations, their expressive language when speaking about a subject of their choosing was quite exceptional. Indeed, he commented with clear fondness that in such contexts the issue was rather bringing the conversation to a close, as their reserves of knowledge on their given subject was seemingly endless – this trait I too am personally and fondly familiar with (Asperger, 1944, translated in Frith, 1991, p. 53). In taking the time to speak to these children, whom Asperger affectionately dubbed 'his little professors', he was able to identify another unique facet of the autistic condition: the 'Special Interest'. The preoccupation with a particular topic remains arguably one of the most easily recognizable traits of Asperger syndrome, or what is now typically referred to as 'high functioning autism'.

For Asperger, however, these special interests were of greater significance than merely establishing shared characteristics in behaviours. He believed that the children's ability to understand and articulate their passions and hobbies in such a way demonstrated beyond refute that they were, indeed, not only educable but socially valuable:

This ability ... can in favourable cases lead to exceptional achievements which others may never attain. Abstraction ability, for instance, is a prerequisite for scientific endeavour.

Indeed, we find numerous autistic individuals amongst distinguished scientists. (Asperger, 1944, translated in Frith, 1991, p. 74)

This perception of autistic intelligence has been both celebrated and criticized for 'romanticizing' the image of the genius savant (Frith, 1991, p. 32). Asperger himself admitted that the maladaptive behaviours associated with autism were indeed much more common (Asperger, 1944, translated in Frith, 1991, p. 74). However, Asperger had reason to portray what was perhaps a rose-tinted view of the condition. For children who had, to all intents and purposes, been deemed lost causes, the significance of Asperger's words could determine their future, and indeed their lives.

This decision to misrepresent the demographic of patients he had observed, while likely well intentioned, left a lasting impact on his research. While arguably promoting inaccurate expectations of the Asperger condition, Asperger also obscured many of the shared characteristics with Kanner's children, who were, in fact, far more representative of Asperger's patients than those he chose to admit. In suppressing some of the more maladaptive symptoms in his patients, Asperger unwittingly distinguished his research from Kanner's and deprived himself from being associated with the discovery of what was, in essence, the same condition.

And yet the dualistic discoveries by Kanner and Asperger of two separate – yet hair-splittingly similar – conditions highlighted potentialities of autism that could not be ignored. As the notoriety of both articles grew, and their similarities became apparent, research began to question whether these men were in fact documenting the same phenomena. Nonetheless, there were sufficient differences so that one could, as Asperger did, draw a distinction between the symptoms displayed in his patients and those of Kanner. How, then, does one account for the existence of two distinct conditions whose symptoms overlap so significantly?

From syndrome to spectrum

Some decades later, Navy psychologist Bernard Rimland raised the question that perhaps Kanner may have been somewhat exclusionary in maintaining such a rigid diagnostic criteria, potentially excluding children who portrayed enough, but not all, of what Kanner deemed autistic behaviours (Rimland, 1965, p. 21).[4] For his part, Kanner criticized what he termed 'the dilution of the concept of early infantile autism', believing that his condition was being diagnosed too readily by other practitioners (Kanner, 1958, p. 110). However, increasing attention was being given to the possibility that autism existed as a condition that varied considerably in severity and symptoms, often presenting in distinctly different ways depending on the individual. Rimland considered that such differentiation represented not different conditions, but in fact suggested the existence of 'sub-groups' of symptoms and ability within the same condition (Rimland, 1965, p. 60).

This theory was later developed by British psychiatrist Lorna Wing (herself a parent of an autistic child) into what we now refer to as 'the spectrum model'. Wing concluded that the variation in the children she observed, and multiplicity of their symptoms could not feasibly be considered to be separate conditions, but rather pointed to a continuum within the autistic condition. Furthermore, she argued that autism was not a static, unchanging condition, but that the patients she observed could be seen to move along this continuum in either direction. She described some patients who initially presented with 'classic autism' who later, following maturation, presented as more firmly within the Asperger category (Wing, 1996, p. 29).

When considered as a spectrum, rather than a fixed, stable entity, autism becomes 'an interpretative category ... not multiple, not bounded, but fluid' (McGuire, 2016, p. 21). While some argue that the expansion of criteria furthers the pathologizing of autistic traits, Wing's contribution arguably not only shaped autism research in highlighting that it could be a diverse and changeable condition, but also altered the way in which we speak of autism. Today, practitioners and parents typically favour the term 'Autism Spectrum Disorder', often abbreviated to 'ASD', rather than the traditional terms of 'autism' or 'Asperger's', which arguably perpetuated narrow diagnostic criteria.

Indeed, in recent years I have personally witnessed a shift in the dialogue with my son's doctors from 'Asperger's' to the broader category 'ASD'. This development highlights that the diagnostic process has now become much more flexible as a consequence of the spectrum model, opening doors to children who may previously have narrowly missed a diagnosis due to the rigidity of traditional autism criteria. However, such developments are not unproblematic. In recognition of the connotations imbued in the use of the word 'disorder', increasingly there is a propensity towards considering the 'autism spectrum' within a framework of 'neurodiversity'. Such language helpfully emphasizes the fluidity and diversity of autism as a condition, while at the same time negating harmful demarcations of difference. Perhaps unwittingly, it also serves to underscore the complications of viewing autism as a clear-cut condition. In what follows, I will continue to unravel the threads of what makes autism particularly difficult to classify, highlighting that such threads are frayed, multi-hued, and somewhat impossible to stitch together.

Notes

1 'Interview with Dr Stephen Shore: Autism Advocate and on the Spectrum', https://ibcces.org/blog/2018/03/23/12748/, accessed 12.03.19.

2 John Elder Robison (2013), 'Ignorance, Autism, and the Things People say', 25 February, *Psychology Today*, available from www. psychologytoday.com/us/blog/my-life-aspergers/201302/ignorance-autism-and-the-things-people-say, accessed 13.05.19.

3 The ICD-10 refers to International Classification of Diseases, tenth edition. Currently the most commonly used diagnostic manual in the UK, this volume draws strongly from the DSM (Diagnostic and Statistical Manual) used in the United States, https://www.autism.org.uk/advice-and-guidance/topics/diagnosis/diagnostic-criteria/all-audiences

4 It is worth noting, though, that Rimland would go on to create his own exhaustive diagnostic checklist that would be adopted by practitioners for some decades, and that was arguably more specific and meticulous (and therefore potentially exclusionary) than Kanner's.

2

Causes for Conflict – Theories as to the Origins of Autism

Perhaps one of the most challenging aspects of autism, for individuals and practitioners alike, is that 70 years later we are no closer to a definitive answer as to exactly how autism comes about. Perhaps as a consequence of this, autism is still very much a condition that is significantly stigmatized for both autistic individuals themselves and their families. With the shadow of 'toxic parenting' still looming over autism, the absence of a clear-cut cause often compels parents to search more fervently for answers. That we still cannot say with any degree of certainty that autism is a neurological, psychological or biological condition leaves the condition vulnerable to misrepresentation and misunderstanding. While there is currently no accepted cause of autism, several theories – of varying merit – have been presented over the years.

Psychological

As we saw in Chapter 1, autism was initially associated with childhood schizophrenia and first documented within the field of psychiatry, where it remained for several decades. Both Kanner and Asperger considered autism to be a form of psychiatric disorder. Today, this theory is considered controversial, as it implies that autism is a form of mental illness, which can be stigmatizing for the autistic individual. Nonetheless, psychological explanations of autism have arguably retained their popularity, as many of the characteristics associated with autism are considered to be relational and behavioural, and therefore more strongly associated with personality.

One of the most prevailing psychological theories of autism is the theory of mind approach, proposed by psychologists such as Michael Rutter (1970) and Simon Baron-Cohen, Leslie and Frith (1985). In their 1985 article 'Does the Autistic child have a theory of mind?', Baron-Cohen, Leslie and Frith found that autistic children consistently failed tests designed to gauge an individual's awareness of the thoughts and motivations of others, in comparison to the neurotypical children and children with Down's Syndrome used as controls. This, they reasoned, accounted for many of the social relational difficulties often found in autistic individuals (Baron-Cohen, Leslie and Frith, 1985, p. 40).

While this theory is useful in attempting to understand the social deficits experienced by the autistic individual, it has faced criticism in recent years for failing to account for the myriad of other symptoms associated with autism that are not social relational (Tager-Flusberg, 2001, p. 186). Katherine Loveland furthers that such an approach confines autism as being located within the person: 'when viewed this way, autism tends to be reified as a thing (a static syndrome or deficit) that afflicts a person and remains throughout life; thus, the person is said to "have autism," rather than to have autistic characteristics or behaviours' (Loveland, 2001, p. 19).

Environmental

In Kanner's seminal study in 1943, we have seen how he considered autism to be a mental health condition, brought on by the absence of a warm and loving family environment. Kanner proposed that these parents busied themselves with instilling information, rather than love, in their children, which accounted not only for their unusual feats of intelligence, but also their social relational difficulties. In echoing the parental fears ignited by Freud's oedipal complex, autism was reduced to a 'psychodynamic conflict' that placed the blame, and consequently hopes for recovery, squarely on the parents (Frith, 2003, p. 30). This hypothesis was enthusiastically adopted by contemporaries such as Bruno Bettelheim, Rudolf Ekstein and Lauretta Bender and became fundamental in shaping treatment and intervention strategies for decades to come (Evans, 2013, p. 9).

This theory has now thankfully been almost universally dismissed; however, the ramifications of this controversial hypothesis were considerable. In positioning autism within the realm of child psychology and family therapy, it arguably discredited autism as a lifelong, developmental condition, hampering any multidisciplinary research for several decades by implying that autism was a mental state from which one could recover. Furthermore, the notion that autism was located within the family was an insidious one. Despite this theory largely being discredited, there is often still a very real sense of culpability and shame felt by parents following a diagnosis (Frith, 2003, p. 30).

Genetic

Hans Asperger also noted peculiarities in the parents of his patients, particularly in relation to their unusual level of education. In contrast to Kanner, Asperger believed that the similar traits observed in families implied a genetic component to autism, observing 'related incipient traits in parents or relatives in *every* single case where it was possible to make a closer acquaintance' (Asperger, 1944, translated in Frith, 1991, p. 84). He also suggested that the overwhelming prevalence in males reinforced the hypothesis that autism was a condition with a strong genetic component, and one that was potentially linked or inherited through gender. This theory has stood the test of time, as it is generally accepted today that autism is a developmental condition that is likely genetic in origin (Tsatsanis and Volkmar, 2001, p. 81).

However, exactly which genes contribute to autism remains an area of research that requires considerable further enquiry.

Catherine Tsatsanis and Fred Volkmar in their examination of neurobiology and genetics in autism observe that:

> ... latent class analysis methods have been used to estimate that probably 2 to 5 genes act in concert to produce an autistic phenotype. However, as many as 10 to 12 genes may be implicated, and it is not predicted that the same genes would consistently be involved. (Tsatsanis and Volkmar, 2001, p. 82)

Recent research from Edinburgh University has succeeded in linking specific genes associated with autism and increased cognitive ability in the general population, particularly in relation to problem-solving tasks (Clarke, Lupton and McIntosh, 2016). However, the multiple ways in which autism can present is problematic when attempting to successfully chart a genetic map of autism. Silberman observes that even the most common markers associated with autism were found in less than 1 per cent of a recent sample study of children, and cites neurogeneticist Stanley Nelson: 'If you had 100 kids with autism, you could have 100 different genetic causes' (Silberman, 2015, p. 15).

Genetically gendered?

Autism has, traditionally, been considered a condition that predominantly affects males. The ratio of boys with autism to girls is generally accepted to be 4:1, with high-functioning autism (or Asperger's syndrome) being even higher at 15:1 (Frith, 2003, p. 64). Asperger himself initially considered the condition that he observed to *only* affect boys, although later modified this to its *rarity* among females (Frith, 2003, p. 64). This perception in relation to boys has arguably endured over the last century, with girls being largely invisible from the autism narrative.

So pervasive has this gendered assumption been that some researchers have suggested that it is in fact a biologically gendered condition. Dr Simon Baron-Cohen, experimental psychologist and autism researcher, has claimed that autism is 'an extreme form of the male brain' (Baron-Cohen, 2002, p. 248). The propensity towards analytical and systemizing thought processes over those that are emotion driven, he argues, are indicative of a higher level of 'male traits', suggesting that autism is the consequence of increased levels of testosterone and other androgens prenatally (p. 248). Similar studies have suggested a link between testosterone levels in childhood in autism symptomology (Auyeung, Baron-Cohen and Ashwin, 2009, p. 20; Knickmeyer, Gross and Baron-Cohen, 2006, p. 830); however, no large-scale medical research has been done with regard to this potential association. It is also worth noting that prevalence of autism in girls has not been shown to correlate with stereotypical 'male' behaviours.

In the context of this research, the sample presented by my participants shows a ratio of two girls to three boys – notably, with one girl and boy being siblings. While this is a particularly small sample, and therefore cannot be used to generalize, the ratio does suggest that autism among girls is more common than is assumed. Emerging research (and accounts from autistic women themselves) have suggested that the diagnostic differential observed between boys and girls could be misleading, with girls potentially being more conscious of 'masking' their maladaptive behaviours in order to fit in than their male counterparts. Thus, girls may display better compensatory learning than boys and may consequently be more difficult to diagnose (Frith, 2003, p. 60). Some of the characteristics of autism, such as increased focus on a particular subject and emotional aloofness, may be characteristics that, particularly in educational settings, are perceived as simply poise and concentration and are therefore behaviours that are praised in girls rather than stigmatized. While the reasons for the gender discrepancy is unclear, the suggestion above highlights that binaried and stereotyped 'gender' characteristics pervade much of the literature, arguably hampering a more nuanced understanding of the autistic experience.

Neurological

With the psychological theories of autism failing to account for how such cognitive differences arise, research has in recent decades shifted towards a developmental psychological approach, combining the fields of psychology with neurobiology to attempt to find causality between biological neural difference and the cognitive processes of the mind (Loveland, 2001, p. 17). In contrast to the 'top down' theories of psychology equating symptoms with behaviour, neurobiological theories offer a 'bottom up' approach, suggesting instead that behavioural and sensory symptoms are a consequence of impaired brain structures (Loveland, 2001, p. 18). A study into the electrical patterns of the brain of autistic individuals of varying symptomology, versus neurotypical controls, found that in two-thirds of their sample the autistic individuals showed different activity across the brain in comparison to controls, and a reduction in activity in the frontal lobe particularly (Tsatsanis and Volkmar, 2001, p. 90).

This correlates with similar studies that have drawn links between impaired executive function in autistic individuals and the temporal limbic and limbic frontal regions of the brain responsible for decision-making, perception and behaviour (Frith, 2003, p. 179; Tsatsanis and Volkmar, 2001, p. 90; Loveland, 2001, p. 28). Frith reinforces a neurobiological theory of autism, proposing that a considerable number of shared features can be seen in the behavioural effects following damage to the frontal areas of the brain, as in acquired brain injuries, and those commonly found in individuals with autism – for example, emotional regulation and repetitive behaviours (Frith, 2003, p. 179). In current research, neurobiological theories have gained significant credibility in assuming an underlying cause in the development of autistic behaviours.

Biological

Biological models of autism have sought to locate the root of autistic behaviours within the body, medicalizing autism as a condition with a biological basis – and, therefore (potentially), biological treatments. In the 1960s, psychologist Bernard Rimland began to get letters from parents of autistic children with alarmingly similar and curious gastrointestinal problems, ranging from diarrhoea, to constipation, to vomiting. As a result, Rimland began research into elimination diets, along with complex regimes of high doses of certain vitamins, which many claimed improved their children's more maladaptive behaviours. Such tests, however, were viewed with scepticism and failed to achieve US Food and Drug Administration approval (Gabriels and Hill, 2002, p. 77).

The potential link between gastrointestinal symptoms and autism was to be revisited with some notoriety in the late 1990s with a controversial study published in *The Lancet* by UK gastroenterologist Dr Andrew Wakefield, which linked 'onset' symptoms of autism with levels of mercury in the blood after children had had the MMR vaccine (Wakefield, 1999). This study has since been widely discredited, with Dr Wakefield having his licence to practise revoked for failing to obtain ethical review and for accepting payment in giving evidence in civil suits pertaining to MMR liability (Holton et al., 2012, p. 691). Although Wakefield's theory was swiftly refuted by the medical community, the impact of the study was manifold. Despite no credible scientific data linking autism to digestion or vitamin deficiency, the association between autism and potential gastrointestinal issues caught the public's attention, particularly among parents who were proactively seeking curative interventions for their children.

In suggesting that autism was a biomedical condition that could be managed, the Wakefield study revived credibility in many untested, costly and arguably dangerous intervention therapies for children (such as induced vomiting and chelation therapy) (Silberman, 2015, p. 80). It also sparked widespread fear and 'anti-vax' movements surrounding the provision of the

MMR to children, with many parents continuing – even now – to opt out of vaccinating their children for fear of 'giving' them autism. This potential link became a focus of fundraising and activism among certain parent groups, most notably 'Autism Speaks'. While such movements that focus on curative interventions have arguably benefited some families in providing access to resources and perhaps a sense of community, they have also been widely condemned in pathologizing and 'othering' autistic individuals by locating their condition within the body as something that has to be overcome and normalized (Waltz, 2013, p. 162).

Comorbidities

A challenging feature of autism is that it is often found to accompany other comorbidities, which can lead to a frustrating and elusive 'chicken or egg' search for answers. Is it that certain health conditions lead to autism, or does autism make someone more susceptible to other health conditions? No one is quite sure; however, there are certain conditions that show markedly more prevalence among individuals with autism. Studies have shown that up to 70 per cent of individuals with autism also have a co-occurring psychological condition (Simonoff et al., 2008, p. 921). Epilepsy and seizure disorders are found to be present in 30 per cent of individuals with autism (Silberman, 2015, p. 199), although rates in the general population fall in the region of between four and ten per 1,000 people.

Particularly in school-age children, ADHD is found to be three times more common among those with an autism diagnosis. While many of the diagnostic criteria for autism and ADHD can be found to overlap, Mayes and colleagues found in a study of 847 children with autism that over half displayed 30 or more symptoms of ADHD, in contrast to the control group of 158 children with a primary diagnosis of ADHD only (none of whom displayed symptoms of autism) (Mayes et al., 2012, p. 278). Tourette's syndrome (or what is now commonly referred to as 'tic disorder'), categorized by involuntary movements, is also associated with autism; however, as with the similarities in characteristics associated with ADHD, researchers do not agree as to whether such movements could instead be described as ritualistic or repetitive behaviour (Baird et al., 2006, p. 211).

Interestingly, both myself and Naomi, also mother to a 12-year-old boy, have children who have a 'comorbid' diagnosis of autism, complicated by ADHD and Tourette's. In Naomi's case, her son was diagnosed with Tourette's in the first instance, followed by ADHD, and then, ultimately, by a diagnosis of ASD. She reflected that she did not remember at any point being advised of the potential assessment of these conditions, but rather that they presented themselves quite obviously during the broader diagnostic assessment. This is consistent with my own experience, in which Micah's supplementary diagnoses were mentioned as almost incidental to his broader diagnosis of ASD. This suggests that their prevalence as part of an ASD diagnosis is particularly common.

What is also interesting is that a 'comorbid' diagnosis can be seen to impact the experience of autism, and indeed the parenting of children with autism, both positively and negatively. That the symptoms of these three conditions can be seen both to overlap, and contradict one another, may arguably exacerbate some of the more complex ASD symptoms, and prove extremely difficult for parents to work out which condition exactly is presenting particular challenges for their child. Naomi said that her child's 'tic' was a physical movement that provoked considerable discomfort for him. While my own son's tics were first identified as verbal (an unusual clucking noise at the back of his throat that I had naively presumed was his attempt to imitate the noise he had heard alligators make at a wildlife park), they have recently becoming ocular – a twitching of his right eye. Micah recently reflected that his tic felt like 'when you need to cough and you can hold it in, but if you do the coughing seems worse when you eventually give in'. The experience of Tourette's is distinctly challenging in this respect, as tics can appear, disappear and reappear without any warning.

However, a 'comorbid' diagnosis also opens the doors to potential support that is otherwise unavailable. Within my specific local authority, there are currently no guidelines for follow-up support from healthcare professionals following a single diagnosis for ASD. In contrast, research into both Tourette's and ADHD have been able to 'medicalize' these conditions to such a degree that there are commonly agreed upon treatment paths and, consequently, support. This presents an unusual paradox in which greater pathologization leads to arguably improved quality of life.

Summary

In this chapter, I have shown how the historical context of autism has strongly influenced how it has been understood, both in the field of research and in society more broadly. Emerging from a period of social tumult, in a climate where research was heavily laden with political agendas, autism arguably had an inauspicious and rocky start in its definition as a diagnosis. These implications served not only to hinder the research process, meaning autism today is still frustratingly ambiguous for researchers and families, but also perpetuated conflicting narratives of what autism is and what it means for the person.

Despite increasing multidisciplinary attention in the last 30 years, the cause of autism and its 'disciplinary home' has still to be established. That there is no consensus as to the origins of autism has meant that some of the more stigmatizing psycho-analytical theories – particularly those placing autism within family dynamics or mental illness – still have roots in the autism debate. Similarly, the indeterminate nature of the condition has left the field open for intervention therapies to persist in focusing on curative treatments, attempting to medicalize autism as a condition that can be overcome.

Part 2 of the book will investigate how these conflicting narratives can be seen to shape both how the diagnostic process unfolds and how it is experienced. While a diagnosis is often presumed to be an end point of uncertainty, the enduring confusion surrounding autism means that diagnosis is in reality the starting point for yet more questions.

'During the first term of this academic year Micah appeared quite settled; his behaviour was not as challenging as it was to become...

"disruptive"
"shouting out, hitting and kicking others and spinning around"
"extreme anxiety"
"exhausted and overwhelmed"
"unable to be contained".'

These words were not unfamiliar to me. They were forever inked on to my thoughts in tears. The term 'challenging behaviour' was a very clean and concise phrasing of a reality that was anything but clean and concise. Our days were uncertain, unsettled, unexpected. There, on the page, was the reality that I was too afraid to speak out loud. If I didn't name those things ... if I didn't speak them ... it wasn't really that bad, was it? He isn't really bad, is he?

Being confronted with those words, in black and white, was a jarring assault on my carefully constructed denial. The last two lines of this report, written by an outreach worker drafted in to untangle the complex knots of behaviour my son had been exhibiting, would pull me out of the deep depths of confusion and despair I had been submerged in, while simultaneously setting me on an unfamiliar road, in the dark, without so much as a map or a torch to guide me.

Having observed Micah over a period of 4 weeks these behaviours appear to be consistent with those described as a 'meltdown' in children with an Autistic Spectrum Disorder. (Date of report: April 2014)

These last lines I read with an almost exuberant sense of relief. There was a reason, a tangible, medical reason, for my son's inexplicable behaviour. It was not my fault. Someone would help us. They would know what to do. Of course, as is so often the case in the complex narratives of an autism diagnosis, it was not that simple.

This remarkable woman, though insightful, was not a doctor. She was not qualified to make such a diagnosis. It was at once given, and at the same time swiftly taken away. I was firmly reminded that:

There is a process to these things. He will need to be fully assessed by a team of multi-agency professionals to establish the veracity of this claim. This may take some time. Until such a point that a diagnosis can be given, we must continue as we are.

Continue as we are. So innocuous, those words. They evoke stability, sameness. Routine. The mundane. There was nothing mundane about our routine. Our routine had become a daily battle to even leave the house, it had become tears and anger and violence, daily phone calls from teaching staff who were as perplexed by his unpredictability as I was. How could we continue like this?

3

The 'Triad': Difference, Distinctions and Diagnosis

As I have sought to articulate, autism is a considerably complex and varied condition in which individual outcomes are unpredictable and uncertain. It is also a condition that is inextricably and complexly rooted in various social, historical and political issues; in other words, what we know about autism has been informed by research shaped by dominant political ideologies that served particular interests. As I have shown in the preceding chapters, although there can be seen to be some shared symptoms displayed by individuals with autism, the ways in which these symptoms present, and indeed the theories as to *why* and *how* they present, are so varied and multitudinous that attempting to categorize autism is almost a contradiction in terms.

Nonetheless, there are certain shared characteristics that are generally seen to be present, and that have informed the criteria currently used to provide a diagnosis of ASD. The World Health Organization has separated these into three – arguably quite broad – sets of diagnostic criteria commonly known as 'the triad of impairments'. For a diagnosis to be made, behaviours from all three criteria have to be observed. In what follows, I will outline the behaviours that are currently considered to fall within these categories, with the aim of demonstrating the breadth, ambiguity and conflicting nature of autism symptoms that make diagnosis particularly challenging.

1 'The presence of abnormal or impaired development that is present before the age of three years'

Although autism continues to be curiously unpredictable in its manifestation, it is now generally agreed that symptoms become apparent very early in infancy and will present in what the World Health Organization terms 'abnormal development'. Childhood development is considered to follow a somewhat linear pattern, albeit there will be some fluidity and fluctuation in development. The attainment of verbal expression, independent mobility, reciprocal actions and object recognition are generally reached by the age of three in typically developing infants. A child may reach each of these milestones at different stages, or at a different rate, within this three-year window. For example, a child may begin their first attempts at speech at nine months, yet not begin to walk until 16 months, and still go on to develop in the same way as any other child.

Consequently, autism is not a condition that is necessarily apparent at birth, or presents itself overnight, but instead very often appears as a series of little irregularities during early development. Sometimes these may be very slight, innocuous even. Different enough to notice, but not quite so different as to cause concern. These inconsistencies build up gradually, though, into a picture of difference that can no longer be ignored. Schulman notes:

> The onset of autism is insidious, not usually marked by the appearance of abrupt or dramatic symptoms. Typically, families experience an awareness that a problem exists, adapting to their child's difficulties without even being aware that they are changing their behaviour and expectations ... The difficulties in diagnosing autism are manifold, as there are no clear or specific biological markers. (Schulman, 2002, p. 25)

Initial concerns are often raised if children are 'not babbling or gesturing by 12 months of age, have no single words by 16 months, have no two-word phrases by 24 months of age, or if any loss of language or social skills is noted' (Schulman, 2002, p. 29). My own son had begun to form words at 9 months and walked at 11 months. He could hold a crayon; he had a healthy appetite. His toilet training was frustrating, but no more so than any other child of this age. His delay in receiving a diagnosis was, in hindsight, in large part hindered by his developing *too* typically. That such variation can be seen even in ordinarily developing children makes it extremely challenging to diagnose autism at this crucial early developmental stage.

The juxtaposition between 'normal' and 'abnormal' development as the primary marker in autism highlights, however, that even in diagnostic terms symptoms are rarely 'value neutral'. In presenting the 'abnormal' versus the 'normal', there is an insinuation that something is 'not quite right'. Anne McGuire takes this further in saying that often such symptoms of child development are framed as 'red flags', 'warning signs' to be looked out for, a threat one needs to be alert to. That such language is commonplace in respect to autism conveys how easily fear and anxiety – and even dread – may take hold of parents and caregivers navigating the diagnostic process. Furthermore, it points to an underlying, and arguably more sinister, bi-product of what McGuire terms 'pathologization' – stigmatization of 'abnormal bodies' (McGuire, 2016, pp. 54–8). As I will go on to show, this can often have more far-reaching consequences than the issue of typical symptoms.

2 'Abnormal' function in communication and reciprocal social action

This second diagnostic category furthers this juxtaposition between the 'normal' and the 'not'. It consists of perhaps the most easily definable and recognizable characteristics of 'classic' autism. It is in this category that it is presumed individuals with autism will experience delays in speech acquisition, generally compounded by an apparent lack of interest or ability in responding to social communication, in addition to unusual speech patterns or inflection. Our desire to communicate with our children, to hear their thoughts and witness their personality develop through verbal actions, is likely to cause parents to be especially vigilant to a lack of social interaction in their children, leading this to be a common early indicator of autistic characteristics.

It is also these particular characteristics that are thought to have inspired the term 'autism'. Coined by Swiss psychiatrist Eugen Bleuler in 1912, the term conjoins the Greek word *autos*, meaning 'of the self', with *ismos*, meaning action or state of being. Literally, it translates as 'being of the self' (Evans, 2013, p. 4). Although originally used to describe a withdrawal from social interaction and self-preoccupation observed in patients with schizophrenia, Kanner adopted this term to describe what he perceived to be a disinterest in the social world and desire for aloneness among his patients (Kanner, 1943, p. 242). This image of autistic children as being vacant, retarded in their development and incapable of understanding human love has remained an enduring one. Autism in popular culture has often been represented as an elusive, rare affliction, associated with institutionalization and lifelong care. The 1988 film *Rain Man* juxtaposes Dustin Hoffman as a middle-aged man with the mental age of a child, despite possessing an incredible 'savant' memory, with Tom Cruise as the handsome and charismatic younger brother.

This representation of autistic individuals as *choosing* to avoid social contact or being indifferent to others' emotions or attention has pervaded perceptions of autism for generations, leading to autistic individuals being considered cold, unfeeling or incapable of emotion (Swinton, 2012b, p. 275; Lawson, 2008, p. 47). This has been a very hurtful and damaging stereotype to the autistic community and has arguably contributed to the many barriers autistic individuals face in respect to social inclusion. Interestingly, Bleuler's observations were conversely created to categorize what he described as a 'mode of thinking', rather than a pathology (Evans, 2013, p. 4). In framing autism in such a way, its difference is not negative, but neutral.

With the increasing interest in autism in the last few decades, recent studies – and indeed accounts from autistic individuals themselves (Grandin, 1996; Shore, 2006) – have supported Bleuler's definition, proposing that the assumed lack of social interaction present in autistic individuals is not a consequence of a desire for solitude, but rather is evidence of a different way of thinking and processing (Lawson, 2008, p. 103).

Wendy Lawson, a psychologist who is herself on the autism spectrum, has described her difficulty in engaging in conversations with others that are outside of the context of her particular set of interests or range of experiences (Lawson, 2008, p. 59). Those who live with or love someone with autism may raise a wry smile at her admission. My son's favourite pastime will be to tell you, in intricate detail, about whatever has captivated his attention at that particular moment in time. We have had wonderfully in-depth discussions about dinosaurs, marine animals, Vikings and, more recently (and admittedly less captivating for me), his latest Xbox game. He does, however, ask with genuine interest about my day, and will do his best to engage with my answer.

We have had to be mindful, however, over the years, that rhetorical devices can present unpredictable and unexpected challenges for Micah. Context is thought to be particularly important to individuals on the autism spectrum, as it is often relied upon to form 'social rules' or expected outcomes to particular situations so that one may anticipate the correct social response. My husband possesses a very dry wit, and his humour sometimes takes Micah several minutes to navigate before he is able to discern the appropriate response. It has been proposed that individuals with autism may struggle with figurative language, in particular metaphoric language, and have a tendency to interpret speech literally (Kanner, 1943, p. 244). Therefore the difficulty in understanding this reciprocal social action could arguably be seen as one of the most problematic aspects of the autistic experience (Grandin, 1996, p. 50).

In theological contexts, it is suggested that this may present an even more significant challenge of interpretation. Professor John Swinton, himself a health practitioner who has spent his career working closely with individuals with various disabilities, invites us to:

> Imagine what it is like. Someone begins to tell you stories about a man dying and being resurrected and living inside of you. Where exactly does he live? Heart? Lungs? Kidneys? What a disturbing thought! Then they tell you that God is here but you cannot see him, although he is in control of your life nevertheless! And such truths for Christians come before anyone suggests that they gouge their eyes out if tempted by lust! With a little bit of empathy, it is not hard to see how complicated and potentially problematic the relationship between religion and the experiences of people with autism spectrum conditions (including high functioning autism and Asperger's syndrome) might be. (Swinton and Trevett, 2009, p. 2)

For my son's part, his own relationship with religion was short-lived. He attended Sunday school for a brief period when he was five or six, as a consequence of my desire to provide opportunities for socialization, and perhaps an unconscious attempt to find some community. He declared upon his return one Sunday that he would not be going back, as, 'They don't believe in dinosaurs, Mama.' That was that. While Swinton, and indeed Micah, highlight the particular challenge that 'faith' may present to 'literal thinkers', in recent years theological reflections from autistic individuals themselves are beginning to emerge which highlight that some of the characteristics of autism can in fact be particularly intuitive to many aspects of religion. Indeed, the familiarity and routine of rituals, prayers and liturgy lend themselves well to the next diagnostic category that I will turn to.

3 Restricted, stereotyped behaviour

Further to difficulty in social interaction, the last category of the diagnostic triad is often considered to be a preoccupation with routines, specific objects, movements, obsessive interests and ritualistic behaviour (Frith, 2003, p. 14). Temple Grandin, autistic writer and engineer, describes in nuanced detail her own 'fixation' on 'ritualistic behaviours' that ultimately diagnosed her as autistic. She recalls being particularly preoccupied with the repetitive action of spinning. Spinning, or other ambulatory movements, are common characteristics of autistic individuals and are generally described as self-stimulatory behaviours or 'stimming':

> Spinning was another favourite activity ... self-stimulatory behaviour made me feel powerful, in control of things ... I realise that non-autistic children enjoy twirling around in a swing, too. The difference is the autistic child is obsessed with the act of spinning. (Grandin, 1996, p. 18)

Like Temple, winding up a swing and allowing it to turn ferociously is one of my son's most beloved pastimes. He has always delighted in any movement that propels him, and spinning is his particular favourite. It is also my particular favourite to watch, as it is when he is at his most carefree and joyful.

Autistic behaviours are often distinguished by their inexplicability to others, and their all-consuming nature to autistic individuals themselves. Indeed, it is the intensity with which autistic individuals adopt certain behaviours that seems to differentiate mere hobby from obsession. At times, this may take the form of a 'special interest' in a particular area. These will vary from individual to individual, although they are often comprised of a subject or object that is quantifiable, predictable and easily systematized (Lawson, 2008, p. 83).

While my son has had a few 'special interests' over the years, the most enduring has been dinosaurs. He has memorized the types, locations and eras of any dinosaur you would care to mention, and in fact he would be quite delighted if you would.

Their size, their diet and their habits have all been carefully catalogued in his brain and are ready to be whipped out at a moment's notice, with the most tenuous, if any, connection to the conversation at hand. I know of another boy who is equally fascinated by trains: their engineering, their weight, speed, fuel. Still another child is fascinated by sugar packets, and fervently collects packets he considers to be unique or interesting to him.

Attention to a restrictive interest falls under the category of 'repetitive behaviours' as it often becomes ritualistic in its manifestation – for example, collecting, cataloguing or memorizing information or objects pertaining to the subject (Kanner, 1943, p. 245). While the impetus towards this behaviour is unknown, a recent study into restricted interests in children with autism has suggested that such behaviour, like stimming, is perhaps a functional tool to inhibit anxiety, and can be seen to be used as both a means of distraction for autistic individuals and as a means of attempting to order or control one's own environment (Spiker et al., 2012, p. 314). Order, routine and an averseness to change is also a pervasive theme in autistic behaviour. Leo Kanner's early observations of autistic behaviour described his patients as having 'limitation in the variety of spontaneous activity' and an 'anxiously obsessive desire for the maintenance of sameness' (Kanner, 1943, p. 246).

While Kanner considered his patients' routines to be almost arbitrary and insignificant, numerous studies since have stressed the importance of consistency and routine to the autistic individual in managing their sense of emotional stability (Gray, 1997, p. 1100). Lawson suggests that in fact every individual is reliant on routines. The problem, she considers, is that autistic routines may appear different or unusual to other people's (Lawson, 2008, p. 87). This unusual feature, coupled with the perception of 'autistic aloofness' discussed in the previous section, can often be seen to form the cultural blueprint of how we perceive autism.

Despite understanding and awareness of autism increasing significantly in the last decade, the portrayal of the clumsy, socially awkward savant remains an attractively enduring metaphor. Although the show's producers have refused to comment on the implied association, Sheldon Cooper of the popular TV show *The Big Bang Theory* has become for many almost a poster boy for the autism spectrum, with his impressive intelligence balanced only by his uncompromising routines, fear of change and inability to intuit social interactions.

While these popular representations vary considerably in their portrayals, they can all be seen to position the autistic individual as 'other' to the central protagonists in these stories – often as clever or amusing plot devices designed to elucidate some moral epiphany (Howell, 2015, p. 151). What is consistent is their arguably one-dimensional illustrations of what is, by all accounts, a very multi-dimensional condition. The reality, as we know, is more complex.

It is this complexity that accounts for the addendum that often accompanies the 'triad of impairments' – 'and other non-specific problems'. This final category of autistic characteristics is undoubtedly the most abstruse and problematic area to navigate, both for professionals involved in the diagnostic process and parents themselves. The phrase 'non-specific' problems, while helpfully grouping an alarmingly wide range of characteristics under a single umbrella, also serves to muddy the waters of exactly what characteristics are, or are not, seen to be autistic. This ambiguity is particularly difficult for caregivers, as it opens up the realm of possibility that any or all behaviours could arguably be defined as 'autistic'. This ambiguity, I will go on to describe, makes the lived experience of parents navigating their way through the diagnostic process particularly challenging.

4

From Uncertainty to …?

Uncertainty is not an emotion, but is a cognitive state of confusion or lack of clarity that tends to generate the emotion of anxiety. In any case, it is the opposite of closure or certainty and the ability to put something out of one's mind associated with it. (Brock, 2019, p. 178)

As I have sought to demonstrate in the preceding chapters, autism is a condition that is characterized by ambiguity and uncertainty. Despite it being commonly accepted that children with autism are considerably more likely to 'develop successfully' the earlier diagnosis and potential intervention takes place (ideally prior to the child turning three), it remains frustratingly difficult for parents to obtain a diagnosis for their children (Zelzazo, 2001, p. 41). Research carried out by Howlin and Asgharian found that of the 770 parents they interviewed concerning the diagnostic process, 60 per cent of their children were not diagnosed until a third diagnostic consultation, with more than 25 per cent being told 'there was no problem' or 'not to worry' at the first appointment (Howlin and Asgharian, 1999, p. 836).

There is a tendency among professionals to adopt a 'wait and see' approach to development so as not to misdiagnose and potentially mislabel a child before they have had the chance to 'outgrow' particular behaviours (Sansosti, Lavik and Sansosti, 2002, p. 87). In this respect, the varying behaviour seen in autism may often function to inhibit its own disclosure, as a very young child may meet some, but not all, of the diagnostic criteria at the point of assessment, or simply be too young to accurately assess in terms of language and cognitive ability, despite showing other early indicators of autism. The diagnostic process can therefore be seen to be hindered twofold. In one respect, this process can be seen to be impeded by parents themselves, who may be reluctant to admit that their child is not developing in the same way as other children. In *Love is Not Enough; A Mother's Memoir of Autism, Madness, and Hope*, Jenny Lexhed, a first-time mother, shared her nagging dread that her son was different from his peers:

> Increasingly, I understand that Lucas is not like other children. He has always been different ... but now the differences are beginning to be so big that they're noticeable. Somewhere in the back of my mind: the word 'autism' is spinning ... but I don't want to believe it's as serious, as terrible as autism. (Lexhed, 2015, p. 17)

Micah was 'the baby' of our family by some 20 years, and so our memory for comparison was limited. At nine months old, however, he forged a bond with another baby at his nursery who was six months older and, as luck would have it, our next door neighbour. That baby became, and remains, a best friend and brother to Micah. They have grown up side by side, yin and yang in nature, perfectly complementing each other in their difference. I can say with absolute conviction that their relationship has helped Micah to navigate the world. Yet it was also their relationship that began to highlight the fact that Micah's own relationship to this world was different.

For the women who have chosen to share their stories, myself included, our spectrum children were all given to us as first-time mothers. The 'first-born' brings with it enormous anxiety, self-doubt and bewilderment as one attempts to navigate being wholly responsible for another human for the first time. But the first-born also sets the benchmark, so to speak, and therefore there is little scope for comparison with what is 'normal'. Despite subtle indications that development was not what it was expected to be, research suggests that the doubt of having no comparison often outweighs the compulsion to seek external advice. Without a frame of reference or a context for appropriate development, the difficulty in reconciling gut feeling with action is a significant one. Clara Claiborne Park, writing of her own journey with autistic daughter 'Elly', articulates the significant challenge of measuring 'normal' development:

> Popularized psychology has encouraged a high level of free-floating anxiety even in the parents of normal children. The situation is made worse by the fact that a disproportionate number of abnormal children in general, and of autistic children in particular, are first children. Their rejection of love is more terrifying because their parents have no experience of the affection of normal children; their bewildering behaviour is, to uncertain and inexperienced mothers and fathers, more bewildering still. It would be hard indeed, in today's climate of opinion, for the parents of a seriously deviant first-born child not to feel they were in some way responsible. (Claiborne Park, 1995, p. 130)

Observing the differences presented by her daughter in comparison to her other three 'beautifully normal' children, Claiborne Park's own frame of reference was coloured by self-denial; the knowledge that she had raised three 'normal' children before reassured her that this child, surely, would be no different:

> So Elly grew, and though we look back and remember one incident or another, the onset of the condition was imperceptible. We perceived we had a child who, at twenty-two months, was not toilet trained – but neither were most of our neighbour's children. She did not walk, but the little boy down the street had sat contentedly in his play pen until he was two ... She spoke only a few words – but the onset of speech in children is notoriously variable, and every parent of a slow talker is aware that Einstein didn't talk until he was four. The various signs that now seem so clear then seemed easily attributable to individual differences. (Claiborne Park, 1995, p. 23)

These attempts to reconcile her daughter's difference comforted her, for a brief while at least, that her daughter too would 'catch up' despite all evidence to the contrary. She writes, poignantly, of her attempts to deceive herself that everything would be 'just fine': 'She would grow and take her place in a family lovelier than anybody else's …' (p. 29). However, as each milestone passed without any indication that it was likely to be achieved, Claiborne Park painfully admits to herself that her dreams of Elly catching up with her thriving siblings would not be realized:

> It is possible to learn humility … A year later, Elly would be examined again, in a bigger hospital with more refined techniques. And this time I would wait at night and hope and nearly pray that they would find a physical deficiency – something that could be controlled with a diet or a pill. And then my baby's perfect health would be a heartbreak to me and no source of pride. (Claiborne Park, 1995, p. 29)

Sansosti, Lavik and Sansosti noted that the majority of children in their study, despite their parents first noticing differences in their development between nine and 12 months, were not officially diagnosed until they were of school age (Sansosti, Lavik and Sansosti, 2012, p. 86). This is alarmingly consistent with my own experience. Initial concerns regarding my son's behaviour were raised in the last 18 months of his preschool nursery placement, and a diagnosis was not formally made until June 2015, 14 months after beginning his assessment, and two to three years after his development presented as 'atypical'. Naomi described her son's diagnostic process as taking 18 months. In our accounts, and throughout the literature, it became clear that it is extremely common for parents to be referred from one professional to another, to still another, in the attempt to obtain a diagnosis. Sansosti and his colleagues noted that 'such a circuitous, redundant undertaking likely is frustrating and may contribute to feelings of uncertainty about the information received and which direction to take' (Sansosti, Lavik and Sansosti, 2012, p. 81).

Speaking with Naomi, mother to an 11-year-old boy with ASD and other comorbidities, she emphasized feelings of self-doubt and uncertainty throughout the diagnostic process:

> You start doubting yourself. Before he was diagnosed, I thought no, maybe there's nothing wrong with him, there's definitely nothing ... and then you think why am I doubting myself, you know there's something wrong. There's so much back and forth ... and then I thought no, there is definitely something underlying. You always get that fear that they'll turn around and say there's nothing wrong and then you won't know.

In sharing her own diagnostic journey, Naomi highlighted a peculiar by-product of this prolonged waiting period – that the frustration and anxiety provoked by such delays may become internalized, leaving mothers questioning whether in fact it is they who have not done enough, or have been too late in recognizing there was a problem:

> Autism didn't even cross my mind to be honest, we just thought he was behind. I feel ... not regret because the outcome wouldn't have been any different, but I feel like I should have picked up on it and I should have picked it up sooner.

She was not alone in struggling with the benefit of hindsight. Despite retrospectively being able to describe in surprising and nuanced detail the early indications of their children's autism, the women I spoke to all expressed regret to some extent that they were unable to identify or act on the signs earlier. Such feelings of regret could also be seen to run heavily through the biographical accounts of Jenny Lexhed and Clara Claiborne Park, who questioned their own effectiveness in advocating strongly enough for their child's diagnosis. For this reason, I have argued that the pre-diagnosis experience of parents is often marked by doubt, uncertainty and fear. The post-diagnostic experience, however, is arguably little different.

5

Diagnosis: A Spectrum of Emotions

I remember a sense of almost professional detachment at Micah's diagnosis. After so many years of ambiguity, I wanted an answer. So desperate was I to end the unknown, I gave little thought to the implications of what that answer might be. After leaving the meeting, I returned home to an empty house and, in the silence, became flooded with all the things I *thought* I knew about autism. I had grown up with the films *Rain Man* and *I Am Sam*, and my experience of autism extended very little beyond these fictitious and cartoonish depictions. Mutism, dependence, inability to form relationships: the worst-case scenarios of spectrum severity, none of which actually represented my son at six years old (nor do they now), flashed before me. I remember sitting on the stairs, helplessly, unable to stop the tears, and mourning the loss of all the things I thought that he would do, that we would do, and which now seemed impossible. He was what I was most proud of in my life. He was smart, he was funny ... affectionate. But what would become of him as an adult if he was indeed autistic? Would he retain the qualities that I so cherished, or would they fade away under the label ascribed to him?

Jenny Lexhed writes candidly, and often painfully, about her emotional journey following her son's diagnosis. She describes the helplessness of being unable to understand or to guide him in his self-imposed isolation from the world, and her sorrow for the loss of all the experiences she fears her son may never have. So severe was Jenny's emotional strain during this period that she was in fact placed under psychiatric restraint, and hospitalized for several months before she was able to return to caring for her son. She admits:

Sometimes during the day, I can't hold it back and my sorrow
takes over. Like a hurricane, it blows the door wide open and
blackest sorrow completely
Rushes in
Washes over me
Drenches me. (Lexhed, 2015, p. 37)

Naomi similarly expressed an acute sense of grief and fear following her son's diagnosis:

> I had set myself up for a diagnosis, but it didn't make it
> any easier when it came ... it really doesn't. I felt like my
> whole world had collapsed. They say Asperger's, ADHD and
> Tourette's Syndrome ... it was like a punch in the gut ... I was
> scared ... not scared ... no, actually I was scared because I
> thought, how am I going to deal with this? It is life changing.
> I didn't realize just how life changing it was. You fear for
> their future ... their whole future flashes before you ... The
> sense of grief when you get the diagnosis is huge because it
> impacts everyone, even his grandparents.

The word 'grief' is a strongly emotive word to use, and it is not
used carelessly here. Traditionally, grief has been considered
a subject for thanatology – the study of death and practices
associated with it – and consequently strongly associated
with bereavement in which grief is considered a response to a
singular event from which we are, in time, expected to recover
(Bowlby, 1960; Kubler-Ross, 1997; DuBose, 1997). Grief
implies loss, and in the case of a very living child this is an
extremely problematic emotion to experience, much less admit.
To date, parental grief, when considered, is explored primarily
in relation to terminal illness in children, sudden loss of a child,
or issues concerning infertility and miscarriage. Such tragedies
are indeed 'losses'. Emerging research, though, is beginning to
point to the experience of *complex* grief among parents and
carers of children whose diagnoses are not terminal, but instead
associated with the challenges of managing illnesses such as
epilepsy, schizophrenia or other lifelong conditions (Eakes,
1995; Whittingham et al., 2012; Brown, 2016).

However, such studies are increasingly moving beyond the traditional model of 'death grief' towards an understanding of grief as a phenomenon that has much more permeable boundaries. Darcy Harris, Associate Professor/Thanatology Coordinator at the Western University in Canada, argues the need for an understanding of loss that moves beyond a single, temporal event towards an interpretation of loss that encompasses such diverse experiences as change in circumstance, lifestyle and perceptions and expectations of the world (Harris, 2019). Harris draws parallels between John Bowlby's early work on childhood attachment and trauma, and Janoff-Bulman's later work on the 'assumptive world', to suggest that any loss can arguably be understood and made sense of as a loss of our assumptions or expectations of the world and where we fit into it.

This connection may be particularly relevant in respect to autism. In the previous section, the challenges faced by parents of children on the spectrum could arguably be framed as tests of our assumptive world. Our changing perception of our children following diagnosis, our changing perception of others based on their response to our child's condition, and also of ourselves and our ability to cope with these challenges are all significant disturbances to the worldview we held pre-diagnosis. Tom Reynolds writes candidly on this sense of 'expectation versus reality', admitting that a significant emotional hurdle is often letting go of the expectations we had for our lives, and our children:

Learning to love my son has meant putting aside presumptions about what love is, what counts for value in a person, what being human entails. This has not been easy. When there is struggle and pain in the process, I admit my first thought is to feel disappointed, cheated, even betrayed by life. Chris's presence ruptures my controlled, planned, and predictable world. I am inclined to think that somehow things have gone awry, pieces scattered in disarray, hopes deferred. Because of this, it is a sense of failure, as if I am flawed in some basic way, have done something terrible to traumatize Chris, or have not done enough to help him accommodate to how a 'normal' child should be, essentially fashioning him in my own image. (Reynolds, 2008, p. 113)

This illusion of the 'normal' child is a difficult one to dispel. Jenny Lexhed describes her joy and pain of attending her son's Christmas nativity, in which the juxtaposition of her own child with all the other angelically 'normal' children was laid bare:

> Sorrow makes itself felt repeatedly ... He can't sit still. I can see how his skin is crawling, he shoves and pushes past the others next to him. Sometimes he calls out to me, and I smile at him, wave, and hold a finger up to my lips, signalling that he needs to be quiet ...
>
> The children sing many Christmas songs ... and amid all the joy I become so sad that I cannot hold back my tears. (Lexhed, 2015, p. 214)

Reading this particular passage brings tears of my own. I myself sat year after year at the same school shows, each time praying this would be the year he would be able to attend. This would be the year I would smile and wave, and he would sing. Yet year after year, he would make it as far as the door into the assembly hall, be confronted by the loudness of the music piping them in, the strangeness of the sea of faces waiting expectantly for him, and abruptly turn and leave. Still, every year, I took time off work, and took my seat. In his last year of primary school, he asked me not to attend. 'There's no point, Mama. I don't want to go, but you being there makes me feel bad about not going.' His words stung more than his empty spot on the stage, and I realized that he too was carrying the weight of unfulfilled expectations.

Naomi shared this sense of sadness at milestones and moments missed – not for herself, but for her son. In considering the reality that he might not be able to achieve 'normal' milestones in life like driving, marriage and children, she reflected:

> And that's okay if they don't ... it's just they won't experience life in the same way that we did. Life won't be simple for

them. You just feel like he should be independent and go on holiday with his pals and me not be worried sick about him. Not be able to go to mainstream ... I feel so much guilt about that because he won't be able to go with his friends who he's so attached to.

Naomi's story strongly resonated with my own sense of grief for all the ways I feared life would be more difficult for Micah. While this was perhaps most acute immediately following his diagnosis, there is an ebb and flow to this particular kind of grief. It can disappear when things are going well, but recur viciously and without warning. A few years ago, I attended a multi-agency review of my son's progress. I had entered that particular meeting armed with discussion points and evidence of my son's progress, which had been steadily improving. I was proud of what he had achieved. We were in a good rhythm, navigating the waters more smoothly. This meeting was to discuss his transition to secondary school, a scary, anxiety-provoking change to our equilibrium. Still, I held on to my belief that he would attend my former school, which I had experienced as a nurturing and supportive place, and where I was certain he would thrive.

In sharing this belief with his review team, I was met with sympathetic, concerned faces. They gently reminded me that while he was indeed doing well, his progress was hard won, and a result of the intensive one-to-one support he had had, and that a mainstream secondary school would not be likely to accommodate. While it was not set in stone, the possibility that he also might not be able to progress up to secondary school with his peers was a very real one. There was also the possibility that this might not indeed even be mine or Micah's choice at all; I was reminded that the 'team around the child' would ultimately decide what they considered to be in his best interests. I was blindsided. I thought he was doing well ... *we* were doing well. And he *was* doing well. So well, in fact, that I had allowed myself not to *forget*, but to place his autism on the margins of our lives rather than at the centre.

I had been deceiving myself that the tenuous equilibrium we

had worked so hard to achieve was evidence that the 'battle was over'. Slowly, insidiously, images of my teenage son had been invading my dreams … of laughing with his friends at the bus stop, worrying about girls, receiving an award at assembly. And in one sentence, those potentialities had been ripped away. I walked out of that meeting arguably more grief-stricken than I had been when he was diagnosed. Hollow and devastated, it was a reminder that expectations can be very dangerous things to hold.

While current research into the emotional journey of parents assumes that 'grief' will be an expected but temporary outcome of diagnosis, our stories indicate that in fact grief is more strongly related to expected 'milestones', which are continual throughout a person's life. Research by Stephanie Brown and colleagues supports this finding, proposing that what is unique to parental grief in respect of childhood disabilities is the continuousness of it. She observes that over time there are recurrent reminders that life will, undoubtedly, be more difficult for your child than it was for you and that this is a constant process of adaptation and adjustment (Brown, 2016, p. 119). The reflections shared here highlight that in fact feelings of grief can therefore be seen to be cyclical, with 'fresh griefs' often recurring years after diagnosis.

This perhaps illustrates that even when what we could define as grief is present, it is a much more complex lived experience than can be reduced to one single event, or even one single emotion. Rather, it is located in multiple sites of 'loss', both present and future, and can manifest in sudden and unexpected ways. In a study by Fernandez and colleagues, it was observed that parents displayed an oscillation of coping mechanisms between 'loss' and 'restoration' following a diagnosis. They observed that parents were continuously adapting to the 'losses' associated with their child's development, while actively concentrating on daily tasks of understanding how best to support their child (Fernandez, 2016, p. 319). In contrast to traditional staged process models of grieving that assume a linear path to a restorative outcome, Stroebe and Schut make clear that in the context of their model:

'restoration' does not refer to an outcome variable, but to secondary sources of, and coping with, stress ... this analysis is focusing on what needs to be dealt with (e.g., social loneliness) and how it is dealt with (e.g., by avoiding solitariness), and not with the result of this process (e.g., restored well-being and social reintegration). (Stroebe and Schut, 1999, p. 214)

This model is arguably resonant with traditional theological paradigms of grief. In theological contexts, this discussion of 'loss' and 'restoration' can be seen to echo theodicies of 'suffering' and 'redemption'. When considered within this framework, 'suffering' is often purported to represent a theological crisis. In the midst of such a 'crisis', the theological temptation is to search for meaning, particularly a meaning that prescribes a redemptive outcome. Melissa Kelly, writing on grief within pastoral care contexts, observes that 'meaning, including theological meaning, helps to create order, sense and purpose out of experiences and events that could otherwise seem random, nonsensical, disordered and chaotic' (Kelly, 2010, p. 75).

This presents as particularly theologically problematic in the context of autism, as autism, by its very nature, is especially 'random, nonsensical and chaotic' to categorize. Furthermore, redemption implies a sense of resolvement, which is an inherently dangerous proposal in respect to lifelong developmental conditions such as autism. Such theologies can arguably be seen to conflate the diagnosed body with the suffering body, inscribing potentially damaging models of suffering as either a personal tragedy or a moral challenge to be overcome (Eiesland, 1994, p. 73). As I have shown, models of suffering that rely on restoration present particular challenges with regard to lifelong developmental conditions such as autism. Furthermore, they imply that autism is a condition that ought to be cured which, for many, is a deeply hurtful rejection of something that is arguably inextricable to their personhood.

In the foreword to John Gillibrand's volume *Disabled Church – Disabled Society: The Implications of Autism for Philosophy, Theology and Politics*, Dr Rowan Williams notes, 'Theologically and socially, we want to "contain" this threatening experience, to reduce people living with autism to problems to be managed.' He cautions, however, that autism is a lived experience 'which doesn't "submit" to the "ordinary" expectations of what can be managed and understood', but instead leads us to a 'wider reflection on making sense, and things failing to make sense' (Gillibrand, 2009, p. 9). Dr Katie Cross, writing of the theological risk in relying on theodicy as a means of simplifying the complex, cautions that: 'All too often, theoretical renderings of theodicy are inapplicable to human experience, pass over the particularities of suffering, and perpetuate a culture of blame. In sum, theodicy can hold greater potential for hurt than for healing' (Cross, 2020).

Rather than the model of 'suffering and redemption', I will go on to argue that in this particular context the dichotomous pairing is rather that of 'grief' to 'relief'.

Loss and restoration: oscillating from grief to relief

Despite research indicating parents are likely to experience an underlying anxiety, and to some extent dread, of receiving a diagnosis, our narratives also reflected that there is significant anxiety that a diagnosis will not be given, and parents will remain in the dark, unable to obtain answers for their child's behaviour. I was equally afraid that we would have no explanation as I was of receiving a diagnosis; that the violence and rigidity and the tears we had grown accustomed to were nothing more than my son being inherently 'a bad boy'. His behaviours were increasingly erratic, unpredictable and challenging, both at home and at school. Pre-diagnosis, my crippling fear that my son was bad at best, 'crazy' at worst, led to a diagnostic label being something that was a much less frightening alternative. Often, as my participants describe, the judgement and stigma experienced by parents attempting to unravel their children's complex symptoms and behaviour creates an unusual paradox in which a diagnosis is both a blow and a relief.

For this reason, it has been my experience that parents often actively *seek* a diagnosis. The diagnosis of autism, rather than an imposed medical authority, or revelation of personal tragedy, is for many parents considered a stamp of legitimacy for what are otherwise deemed to be stigmatizing behaviours. Not only does a diagnosis 'explain' such behaviours, it may open doorways to accessing support, individual education plans, even financial aid. After the seemingly interminable limbo often experienced pre-diagnosis in which families are paralysed from taking steps to improve their child's position, Scarlet, mother to a ten-year-old daughter with ASD, felt liberated by the ability to take some control and responsibility for her children's future outcomes. She explained:

> I was happy to get the diagnosis. It had been a fight to get it ... people say nothing will change but things do change. You get a voice. You can talk till you're blue in the face but without that piece of paper nothing gets put in place. And I don't care what they say, they don't do anything unless they're legally obliged to. I don't have a formal education but I'm articulate and I know how to fight my case, and once we had that piece of paper I was able to fight for what she needed in school. In hindsight I was so relieved to get the diagnosis because I could stop the teachers treating my child as bad.

Scarlet's sense of empowerment afforded her by obtaining a diagnosis and undertaking her own research into how best to support her daughter was palpable. For her, it was affirmation that her doubts were not unfounded, and her efforts to achieve support for her daughter were not in vain. For my part, the (relative, and arguably deceptive) certainty afforded by the confirmation provided tangible relief from a life of uncertainty that I had found so difficult to navigate. I am a person who does not do well with unknowns. I am an over-thinker; the possibility of limitless outcomes provokes acute anxiety in me. It also leads to relentless self-criticism if I had done this, would it still be that? If I do that, what about this? Such a personality, I have learned, is not a winning combination for a parent of a child on the spectrum. As Brock shrewdly observes:

Caring for an autistic child is rife with social ambiguities that burst into view soon after diagnosis. The complexities compound as they spiral out into other domains of lived existence and produce emotional reactions. These social ambiguities and the emotions they provoke deserve closer attention. (Brock, 2019, p. 174)

Micah's diagnosis, I naively believed at the time, would be something that would provide parameters in which I could orient myself. It would quieten the nagging doubts. I was a firm believer in the power of knowledge – I would read the books, I would do my research, I would make the calls, and our path would become clearer. However, receiving a diagnosis, I was to learn, seemed in fact to raise more questions than it answered.

6

'The Power of Naming': Who Wears the Label?

In *Wondrously Wounded*, Brian Brock describes his own and his wife's initial reluctance, and indeed refusal, to obtain a formal diagnosis for their son, Adam. He recalls in painful detail the pressure they felt as a couple from medical professionals, from family, from friends, to agree to a diagnostic assessment. Their reasons not to were multi-faceted, but Brock repeatedly stresses that their touchstone for this decision was the question, 'Will this benefit Adam?' Brock admits that their eventual acquiescence to agree to a diagnosis was a result of a purer need – to end ambiguity in order to access understanding and support. 'Social norms had ground us down,' he remarks, 'Our decision rested on the much messier and less defensible sense that the test would provide social security benefits primarily to Adam's harried parents' (Brock, 2019, p. 70).

Diagnosis, Brock argues, is historically a means by which medical professionals seek to classify symptoms in order to arrive at the appropriate therapeutic treatment, or cure. In the case of autism, there are currently no universally agreed upon therapeutic interventions that can be seen to meaningfully or substantially impact the individual with autism. The variety of symptoms almost precludes success in this task; while one form of 'therapy' or support may be useful for one individual, the same could prove counterintuitive for another. Rather, as Brock candidly admits, obtaining a diagnosis most often serves the parents rather than the child.

In my professional capacity, I am often called upon to contribute to the assessment of children who may likely be on the autism spectrum. I have worked with many children who have presented with very clear indicators that might support a diagnosis, but yet were confident, thriving in their learning, and able to make social connections. They were happy. More than once I have affirmed evidence of ASD characteristics with the caveat, 'The benefit of a diagnosis, however, must be balanced against the benefit to the child.' Scarlet remarked on one professional who, while admitting her daughter fit the criteria, refused to provide a diagnosis, imploring, 'Please don't label her.'

While I personally would never attempt to actively dissuade a family from obtaining a diagnosis, the question of who such a 'label' benefits is an interesting one in respect to autism. My husband shares this discomfort with labels. 'He's just who he is', he often remarks of Micah. Indeed, his complete acceptance of Micah, just as he is, is something I am eternally grateful for. And he *is* just who he is. His autism, however, is also inextricable from who he is. There is arguably not one without the other. In the absence of an affirmative answer to the question, 'Will this benefit the child?', what shone through in Brock's account was the sense that seeking diagnosis would betray a lack of acceptance of their son as who he was.

The discomfort, reluctance and anxiety revealed in relation to diagnosis points to a deeper, and more insidious, relationship between diagnosis and the concept of 'labelling'. Labels, as I will go on to articulate, are rarely value-neutral, but rather are morally charged and imbued with social meanings. Nancy Eiesland, in her volume *The Disabled God: Toward a Liberatory Theology of Disability*, reminds us that, 'the act of naming someone or something grants the namer power over the named. Historically, rather than naming ourselves, the disabled have been named by medical and scientific professionals or by people who have denied our full personhood' (Eiesland, 1994, p. 25).

Eiesland's observation of the power of naming highlights the paradoxical nature of diagnoses, and the conflicting emotions that inevitably follow. On the one hand, as I have described, the 'labelling' by medical professionals absolves parents of the peculiar sense of blame associated with 'abnormal' development, and affords entry into networks of support. However, Brock elucidates:

> The labels parents apply to children matter a great deal for how they learn to position themselves within their social worlds. A diagnosis of a learning disability at least promises the social support a child needs and deserves in order to reach their fullest potential. But to secure that treatment their parents and caregivers will not only need medical certification but will have to learn to describe them in the most negative possible light, as incapable, as falling short, as miles away from the goals of normalcy, and therefore, in important respects, a burden to society. (Brock, 2019, p. 174)

When beginning the process of getting support for Micah, I was advised to 'write his very worst day'. I must caveat here that my child is considered to be on the 'high functioning' end of the autistic spectrum, as are the children of the other mothers who have shared their experiences in this book. Therefore our experiences are undoubtedly different from those considered to be more 'severely' impacted. While my son's very worst days were sometimes very bad indeed, they were not comparable to the 'worsts' others might experience, and were far from a constant. Yet his, and my, opportunity to gain support depended on him being portrayed as such. Thus, while opening doors to support, such a label inevitably opens another door, which, once passed through, is very difficult to close.

A diagnosis of autism transforms the 'named' from an assumed 'normal' into an 'abnormal' state of personhood – he or she becomes, in medical and political terms, disabled.[1] In being so labelled, an individual's lived experience becomes not only shaped by their condition, but by their 'dis-abled' position in an 'able' social world. In the following chapter, I will go on to explore how the label of 'disability' has come to be charged with such social and moral implications, reflecting on how schemas of 'normalcy' have been constructed to create the dichotomy of 'normal' person and the 'abnormal' disabled.

Note

1 There are a multitude of terms used to describe both autism and those with an autism diagnosis. While 'Autism' and 'Asperger's' were initially thought to be separate diagnoses, increasingly these terms are being used interchangeably to describe what is now commonly referred to as ASD (Autism Spectrum Disorder). It is important to note that there are varying viewpoints concerning appropriate terminology for describing people with autism (see Kenny et al., 2016, 'Which Terms Should be Used to Describe Autism? Perspectives from the UK Autism Community'). Anne McGuire challenges the use of 'person with autism' as she proposes that it excises it from the person, reducing it to a pathological entity – 'not "someone", but "something" we don't have to have around' (McGuire, 2016, p. 7). While I myself advocate and believe for a more person-centred construction of autism as being inextricable from the person themselves, for my own personal reasons I struggle with the word 'autistic'. For me, it does not have the same liberatory context in conveying a sense of identity rather than pathology. Rather, I hear echoes in it of 'otherness', of the fictional portrayals that have so deeply harmed the autism community. I realize that this is perhaps anachronistic to my use of 'person with autism'. But that is how my son describes himself, in the same way that he would say he has blue eyes or brown hair. For him it is an attribute of his person, neither negative nor positive. Given that I am representing a multitude of voices in this book, I do not adopt any one term but rather use a full 'spectrum' of terms interchangeably to reflect the diversity of opinions and research relating to the definition of autism.

PART 2

Disability, Normalcy and Stigma

A strange mix of anticipation, dread and relief wrestled for position inside of my chest. Today Micah would begin his new childcare, a service designed for children with additional support needs. He had been unable to cope with mainstream childcare or, rather, they had been unable to cope with him. Understaffed and overwhelmed, they had never learned his language. The almost daily phone calls to retrieve him, at first concerned, later becoming frustrated and impatient, had built up. 'We are not equipped to deal with children like him,' they brusquely reminded me.

My tenuous grip on my job was beginning to slip, my constant absence noticed. Well-meaning line managers expressed their concern. What can we do to support you? they asked. The answer, it seemed, was very little. I could not reduce my hours, nor condense them. I could not work from home. Even if I could, I could not feasibly predict a working pattern around a meltdown. I moved through my days coiled with apprehension, poised for the next phone call.

This new provider, they assured me, would not call. They were used to managing complex behaviour. They had fewer children, more staff. They were very much 'equipped to deal with him'. Even better, they would pick him up and drop him off. My relief was palpable, but precarious. Such 'fixes', I knew, were never as simple as they seemed.

The bus arrived shortly before 9 a.m. 'Ready, buddy?'
'Mmm.'

I slid his tiny backpack over his shoulders, mentally preparing myself as I opened the door for him to not, in fact, be ready to board this bus of strangers. Yet his little feet walked purposefully down the path to the bus door, pausing before climbing on. 'OK. Bye, Mum.'

'Bye, baby! Have a great day!' I beamed.

As the door slid shut, and he settled himself in on a seat much too big for him, I exhaled. He's OK, I thought. He's actually OK. This is going to work.

I slid my gaze along the side of the bus, continuing to smile and wave at the children he would be spending his days with. My smile faltered, my sense of relief plummeted like a stone thrown into a well. The other faces gazing from behind the glass did not smile back. The children's range of needs was diverse, they had explained. Some were quite profound. So consumed was I with my own need that I had not fully considered what this meant. Naively, I was encouraged by this – Micah's difference would be understood here. He would be respected.

But now, gazing at the collection of children before me, whose needs were indeed profound, I was struck by a wave of sadness that was both piercing and unexpected. A memory assaulted me of my own schooldays, when my classmates would run alongside a bus just like this one as it drove by, pulling faces and chanting, 'It's the special bus!'

Special, for them, did not mean precious. It meant different. Lesser. Pitiable.

And as I stood in silent anguish, waving at my own child's face behind that same glass, I realized that they would think he was different too.

7

Disability and the 'Other': The Social Construction of Normalcy

> 'Disability' is a commonplace term. Its meaning, at one level, is beguilingly obvious – not being able to do something. In lay terms, referring to people with impairments – as disabled – signals that they belong to that group of people who cannot engage in 'normal' activities because of their 'abnormal' bodily or intellectual 'deficit' or 'incapacity'. (Thomas, 2002, p. 38)

Disability has occupied a problematic space in our social history. Despite the fact that we all, at some point in our lives, will likely (at least temporarily) incur some form of disablement, the role of the disabled individual has been that of the outsider, as peripheral to the successful functioning of society. Disability theorist Lennard Davis contends that 'the "problem" with disability is not the person with an impairment; the problem is the way that normalcy is constructed in our society to create the "problem" of the disabled person' (Davis, 2013, p. 3).

The term 'disability', much like autism, is thus a simple designation for what is anything but a simple concept. If we are to consider the multiplicity of individuals who identify as 'disabled' and the myriad of conditions and impairments that fall under this over-arching term, the possibilities of variation within this one classification appear infinite. A double amputee, for example, would be considered as an individual with a disability. Such an impairment would be visible, obvious, and would likely be accompanied by physical symptoms of pain or discomfort that would impact an individual's daily life and ability to perform everyday tasks to a considerable degree.

However, we might also be likely to consider someone with autism (who is able-bodied) to have a disability. While the person with autism may not be physically impaired, their experience of the social world is often described as extremely disabling. Their disability, on the other hand, would to a large extent be 'invisible'; it would not be defined by their physicality or rooted in their body to the same degree, and would arguably go unnoticed by the casual observer. Therefore, these individuals' experiences of the world would be wildly different, and yet they would be bracketed under the same 'catch-all' designation for a group of people whose only common characteristic is arguably their 'otherness' to our 'normalness'.

The framing of 'disability' as a collective noun for what are arguably un-collectable impairments has gradually begun to be problematized as overly simplistic, static and discriminatory (Swinton, 2012a, p. 175). In recent decades, the notion of disability has been increasingly challenged as homogenizing a collective condition that does not, in fact, exist. There is no unitary group of the 'disabled' that can be seen to share the same characteristics. This is perhaps no more true than in the case of autism. Rather, the only common characteristic that can be seen to be shared is that individuals with autism may be similarly considered to fall outside the parameters of what is 'normal'. However, this categorization, while seemingly straightforward, has come to raise more questions than it answers. What do we consider as 'normal'? Where did those parameters come from? Who gets to decide who is normal, and who is not?

Being subject to the category of the 'other' is perhaps one of the only truly universal, and most enduring, aspects of 'disability'. Disabled individuals, in the absence of common characteristics in condition, are thus defined by what they are not: not able-bodied, non-seeing, non-hearing, not normal. Davis suggests that 'when we think of bodies, in a society where the concept of the norm is operative, then people with disabilities will be thought of as deviants' (Davies, 2013, p. 8). This distinction between 'normal' and 'abnormal', then, naturally functions to exclude, ignore or devalue the experience of disabled individuals within society. As a consequence, the 'disabled story' throughout history has been one of marginalization, vilification and institutionalization.

Michel Foucault defines this phenomenon as 'biopower', one that is enacted by authoritative (medical) forces who exert physical and social control over 'deviant bodies'. Bodies, he argued, rather than naturally predetermined organic entities, were sites upon which external social forces such as discipline could be enacted (Foucault, 1978, p. 144). In her volume *Feminist Disability Studies*, Kim Hall suggests that many of the issues raised in disability studies are in fact issues that feminism has been attempting to unravel for decades, such as the issues of bodily difference and the regulation of 'different' bodies (Hall, 2011, p. 6). Writing on the integration of feminist theory within disability studies, Rosemarie Garland-Thomson proposes that a feminist analysis offers a particularly strong critique of the material practices, such as medicine, that function to control and 'discipline' bodies of difference (Garland-Thomson, 2011, p. 17).

Theologies that focus on disability highlight that, within the Christian tradition, disabled bodies are often constructed as 'deficient' or 'less valuable' than non-disabled bodies. In her introduction to Nancy Eiesland's *The Disabled God*, Rebecca Chopp observes that despite the 'astounding fact ... that Christians do not have an able-bodied God as their primal image' (Eiesland, 1994, p. 11), there remains a tendency to treat persons with disabilities with a mixture of pity, suspicion and aversion. Such positions assert that Christian theology has all too readily adopted normative, secular, medical models of the body that exalt bodily perfection, and position the wounded, disabled or suffering body as deviant.

The reduction of disability to merely the dysfunctional body, and a body that – as Davis contends – is considered a site of deviance, also functioned to rationalize any stigma or discrimination faced by the impaired as being created, in effect, by their own body. Erving Goffman reminds us that 'stigma' has in its roots a deeply entrenched association with the body; its original use by the Greeks referred to physical symbols on the body to demarcate the bad or the amoral in society (Goffman, 1990, p. 11). Thus, bodily difference, such as disability, has been inherently associated with deviance, immorality and shame (p. 24).

Normal bodies, worth-y bodies

Medical ethicist and theologian Stanley Hauerwas proposes that medicine and religion have always been intertwined, with issues of disease and disability often traditionally considered as much a religious problem as a medical one, arising 'from the disfavour of the Gods' (Hauerwas, 2005, p. 542). However, he contends that at some point along the way medicine has surpassed religion as the institution in which society places its utmost trust in. While medicine promises health and healing in the present and on earth, religion offers the misty promise of salvation in the kingdom of heaven. Faced with such a choice, moral and ethical concerns that had traditionally fallen into the hands of religion are instead increasingly considered within the scope of medicine to address (Hauerwas, 2005, p. 546).

This, he says further, is particularly problematic when we assume that medical authority represents a moral neutrality in society. While he acknowledges that doctors should, and very often do, hold patients' best interests at heart, he contends that what they consider to be 'best interests' are never a-social or a-historical, but rather shaped by what society deems to be valuable at the time (Hauerwas, 2005, p. 559). Thus, he critiques the influence of post-industrial schemas of normativity in contributing to medical models that are centred on prevention, cure and restoration of the socially valuable 'normal body'.

While the marginalization of disabled lives is by no means a modern phenomenon, Paul Abberley points to the changing division of labour in the Industrial Revolution in constructing a society in which social roles, and therefore social value, became inextricably bound with production (Abberley, 2002, p. 125). With large-scale industry demanding consistent and predictable levels of production, the notion of the 'perfect worker' became one in which 'average' was the ideal (Oliver, 1990, p. 46; Thomas, 2002, p. 61). Both disability theorists and theologians have critiqued the influence of dominant capitalist ideologies in defining the 'ideal body' as one that is economically valuable.

This had significant implications for disabled individuals. In a society in which social value was intrinsically linked to production value, being excluded from the labour market meant being excluded from active participation in society. Drawing on Lennard Davis's description of disability as an 'economically generated category' (Davis, 2013, p. 3), post-colonial theorist Sharon Betcher develops this position to suggest that the Church's idealism of the normative body betrays acquiescence to precisely these dominant capitalist ideologies, as critiqued by Marxian and Weberian perspectives (Betcher, 2007, p. 12).

Reynolds proposes that such attitudes within the Church can be seen to be shaped by traditional theologies that rely on medicalized models of disability. In what he defines as the 'cult of normalcy', he asserts that Christian theology has all too readily adopted normative secular, medical models of the body that exalt bodily perfection. Developing Rosemarie Garland-Thomson's critique of modernity, Betcher argues further that parallel to the construction of the ideal body as a healthy body, this also brought into existence a damaging view of suffering, emptying it of meaning and viewing it as something to be eradicated or cured, being that the suffering body was seen as 'deviant'.

In 1951, the sociologist Talcott Parsons proposed that bodies were socially interdependent entities and when such bodies became 'damaged', disabled or sick, they created a 'break in the chain' of reciprocal social action. As a means of bridging this fault in the chain, Parsons proposed the creation of the 'sick role' – a social position that functioned to create a (temporary) space in which individuals were exempt from their social duties under medical advice. After dutifully following this advice, they could be reinstated to their full participation in society (Parsons, 1951, p. 439). Central to this model was the importance of the role of the medical professional, in both legitimizing a person as 'sick', and in providing the tools with which they could 'become better'. However, for individuals with 'impairments', this was particularly problematic, as once diagnosed with an impairment they occupied the 'sick role'. If such an impairment was permanent, the secondary obligation to rehabilitate could not be fulfilled, and therefore the reciprocal social exchange was broken. Without the hope of rehabilitation, the impaired individual remained stuck in a position of 'deviance', dependent on medical professionals for legitimization.

Advancements in medicine and the introduction of vaccinations brought increased life expectancy and the potential for individuals with disabilities to live beyond infancy. However, this itself was not unproblematic. The economic changes brought about by the Industrial Revolution had significantly altered social relationships, with labour migration influencing the emergence of the nuclear family unit and the dissolution of wider familial ties. While individuals with disabilities were now afforded a better chance of survival, they were also now dependent on a much smaller family unit, and much more visible to a society that increasingly considered them superfluous (Thomas, 2010, p. 37). This increased visibility of the disabled person within society made disabilities or any deviation from the 'norm' even more pronounced.

With the additional economic pressures associated with increased life expectancy, and the stigmatization of 'deviance' associated with individuals with impairments, the late nineteenth century also gave rise to the introduction of institutionalization. Families of individuals with disabilities, whose 'social obligation' could not be fulfilled, were encouraged to relinquish their 'financial burdens' to the state, which had begun the process of spatially isolating individuals with impairments from society. At the same time, biomedicine began to develop a model of care in which the primary concern for illness and impairment was 'detection, avoidance, elimination, treatment and classification' (Thomas, 2002, p. 40). It is interesting to note that among these five options, only one concerns the practical management of symptoms; the remaining four are chiefly concerned with the cataloguing and eradication of 'abnormalities'.

Davis highlights that the same statisticians (Adolphe Quetelet, Sir Francis Galton and John Darwin) who promoted the concept of 'normalcy' in their social categorizations were also eugenicists. With this in mind, the statistical classification of humans takes on a sinister and different function: one that is designed to single out, and subsequently remove, the flawed and imperfect (Davis, 2013, p. 9). With elimination rather than amelioration the aim with regard to impairment, institutional life brought with it practices such as enforced sterilization of impaired individuals to prevent the continuation of hereditary conditions (Hauerwas, 2005, p. 151).

The disturbing growth in popularity of the eugenicist movement, coupled with the introduction of institutionalization, meant that individuals with impairments were not only removed from being visible, but that this invisibility also functioned to conceal the practices occurring within institutions. Emphasizing the influence of political ideologies in shaping such dangerously oppressive social policies towards disability, Betcher highlights the very real and dangerous potential of 'normalcy' to function as a form of social violence (Betcher, 2007, p. 160). In the next chapter, I will explore how such violence can be shown to profoundly shape people's view of autism in our society.

8

Autism, Disability and 'Lives Unworthy'

During the time of Asperger's research, Europe was in the midst of World War Two. Vienna, while home to many prominent scientists and intellectuals of the time, was also home to significant Nazi support. This presented a very real danger to research being conducted at the time – financially, morally and physically. The expectation was undeniable; any valuable contribution to science or the arts was to be made under the banner of Hitler's regime, and be representative of their agenda. Building upon ideas espoused in earlier decades by Catholic theologian Josef Mayer, who believed that the mentally ill, poor and handicapped were 'life unworthy of life', Hitler's position on genetic and racial superiority, which had hitherto been raised as a purely theoretical debate, were fast in danger of becoming social policy.

In 1939, one of Hitler's doctors, Theo Morell, produced a paper detailing the financial burden on the state of individuals with disabilities, and introduced a Bill that required the registration of all births with diagnosed defects or disabilities. Within a few short years, this Bill had been utilized to facilitate the 'therapeutic euthanasia' of 336 children in Am Spiegelgrund, the Austrian hospital to which Asperger's Heilpädagogik clinic was attached (Silberman, 2015, p. 143). By the time he presented his paper on autistic disturbances in children in 1944, Asperger was facing an audience of peers who had adopted this model of a 'national socialist medicine'. Asperger was forced to walk a precarious tightrope between appearing to toe the line with his Nazi benefactors and fighting to save the lives of his 'little professors'. His decision to present only his less severe cases, and stress their unusual capacity for intelligence, was arguably driven by his desire to portray his patients as socially valuable, protecting them from what would undoubtedly have been a grim fate.

The unequal power relationship between the individual and the practitioner remains a complex and controversial issue. While we are moving away (albeit only in the last few decades) from institutional models of care, individuals remain hugely dependent on the diagnosis of a medical professional for access to resources, treatment and support. The eugenicist legacy of 'amelioration or elimination' is arguably still strongly resonant in restorative models of medical care. John Gillibrand remarks that, 'Within the United Kingdom, within living memory, the treatment of those with learning disabilities and/or mental health problems, although in no way reaching to the supreme cruelty of the Nazi regime, has not brought credit to our society' (Gillibrand, 2009, p. 160).

Anne McGuire, in her seminal volume *War on Autism*, cautions that despite the years that have elapsed, we exist in 'remnants of a culture that understands itself to be living with autism, but that wishes itself to – and works to – live without it' (McGuire, 2016, p. 20). In what can perhaps be described as chilling echoes of the acts of 'euthanasia' carried out by the Nazi regime, McGuire opens by describing the death of two autistic children in Ontario, Canada, in 2009: Jeremy Bostick and Tony Khor. Both boys were murdered by their parents. The idea that children may find themselves in mortal danger from the very people who are presumed to value their safety above all others is difficult to comprehend. However, McGuire highlights that the press coverage of the murders seemed to encourage us to do precisely that: render the 'unthinkable, thinkable' (McGuire, 2016, p. 9). News coverage of the deaths described the boys' parents as 'devoted', emphasizing the severity of challenges their children presented, and summarizing their murders as 'heartbreakingly tragic'. The emphasis was clear. The parents were similarly victims of a crime; the crime itself being autism.

In 2006, American Republican Senator Rick Santorum proclaimed autism to be an 'urgent public health crisis', devoting sizeable funds to research, detection, prevention and cure. This initiative was to be termed the Combating Autism Act. In depicting autism as a 'war' or a 'crisis', the expense and economic burden of autism was underscored, emphasizing the need to restore the country to a 'peacetime' state of prosperity. However, in framing autism in such a way, there is also the dangerous assumption that such a 'fight' might yield success. As I briefly touched upon in Chapter 2, such a pledge arguably serves to promote to parents unproven, and often very dangerous, 'treatments' or 'cures'. This 'business', as Anne McGuire calls it, is often prohibitively expensive, capitalizing on the desperation of parents who will pay whatever it takes to 'make their child well' (McGuire, 2016, p. 152). I often find myself viewing 'suggested posts' about autism on social media, frequently touting extremely costly (and clinically unregulated) vitamin regimes designed to make your child's autistic symptoms 'disappear'.

This notion of 'disappearance' is insidiously paradoxical within autism narratives. At the same time as 'curative remedies' promise to erase all signs of autism, autism itself is presented as something that 'erases' your child's potential. McGuire paints a vivid picture of the public relations campaign for autism awareness at the 2007 Child Study Center in New York. The campaign featured child ransom posters, with captions such as 'We have your son'. Such images were powerful, conveying in simple black and white the threat of autism as something that might 'steal' our otherwise healthy, innocent, perfect children (McGuire, 2016, p. 126). They also convey that by virtue of its perceived 'invisibility', autism is perhaps dangerously easy to weaponize as something separate, and therefore extricable, from the person. In what follows, I will examine how such schemas function to 'other' and stigmatize autistic lives and, by extension, those who love them.

9

Autism, Invisibility and the Problem of 'Passing'

Disability is so much more than a medically diagnosed impairment, a social stigma, or political activism engaged in the fight against manifest injustice: it is an existential struggle. Foregrounding this personal struggle is theologically important because most people do not find disability disturbing in this deeper and more personal way ... I write then for those who have for some reason found themselves forced genuinely to wrestle with disability. (Brock, 2019, p. xvii)

In previous chapters, I have sought to articulate what this experience of 'wrestling' is like for those of us whose lives are touched by disability in such a deep and more personal way. I have situated autism as a condition that is strongly shaped by social and political attitudes and policies towards disability, and yet which simultaneously defies many commonly held beliefs about what it means to be disabled. It is both rooted in the everyday reality of autistic lives, and yet it is invisible to the lives of others until it disrupts and subverts our social expectations of what is considered 'normal behaviour'.

Autism is, by nature, an invisible condition. In contrast to the differences that are often visually recognizable in the case of physical disabilities, intellectual or developmental conditions such as autism present by their difference in behaviour. Erving Goffman posited that stigmatizing conditions that are 'invisible' (such as autism) allow for the phenomenon of 'passing' as 'normal' in social situations, therefore mitigating others' awareness of their stigmatizing characteristics and allowing for greater opportunities for social inclusion (Goffman, 1990, p. 92). From this, we could infer that the 'invisibility' of autism leads to it being a much less stigmatizing, and therefore less marginalized, lived experience.

However, as Asperger's attempts to shape his research to protect his 'little professors' has shown, the invisibility of autism far from translates into social acceptance. As I have touched upon in the previous chapter, the association of autism with psychological disturbance has left an indelible mark on how autism is perceived socially. In Chapter 1, I illustrated how constructions of 'normal' (and consequently 'abnormal') behaviour have functioned to position difference as inherently suspicious, deviant or pitiable, particularly in relation to cognitive difference. More significantly, the influence of the eugenic beliefs examined in Chapter 2 on social attitudes and policies towards difference made 'normal' a particularly dangerous category to be excluded from when autism was first identified. While we have mercifully moved beyond the devastating reach of social eugenics today, shifts in attitudes are much slower. Although autism is a condition that is considered invisible, and thus affording individuals with autism the 'privilege' of passing as 'normal', it is a condition that also presents very real and tangible barriers to inclusion and participation in social settings.

While normative assumptions of the (adult) body have been critically challenged in sociological inquiry (Goffman, 1990, p. 11; Butler, 1999, p. 47; Davis, 2013, p. 8), children's bodies remain measured against universalized and taken-for-granted assumptions of 'normal' development. In their volume *Approaching Disability*, Katherine Runswick-Cole and Rebecca Mallett suggest that the myth of a unitary collective of experience is particularly evident in the treatment of disabled children in disability studies (Runswick-Cole and Mallett, 2014, p. 39). If we are to consider that disability theory mainly relates, as we have already discussed, first to male experience, with the female experience existing on the margins, then the experience of children is largely missing from the page altogether. Strongly influenced by developmental psychology, children are assumed to follow a linear, staged pattern of development (Burack, et al., 2001, p. 11; Zelazo, 2001, p. 49). This assumed process of 'normal' child development thus inevitably functions to situate anything outside this conventional model as 'abnormal' – immediately pathologizing such a child as 'disabled'.

Anne McGuire observes that there is a peculiar focus on the child in relation to autism. Support literature, resources and social groups are often, if not predominantly, geared towards children. While perhaps this is a legacy from Kanner's depiction of the 'disordered child', nonetheless the notion that autism is a condition of childhood has remained strong. Yet children become adults. Autism is not a fatal condition that will prevent children from reaching adulthood, nor is it a temporary state that they will 'grow out of' (McGuire, 2016, p. 119).

Erving Goffman argues that for children with disabilities, the experience of childhood is complexly and precariously dependent on how their impairment is socially perceived. He suggests that 'a child with a stigma can pass in a special way. Parents, knowing of their child's stigmatic condition, may encapsulate him with domestic acceptance and ignorance of what he is going to have to become' (Goffman, 1990, p. 113). He argues that children already occupy a position of partial social invisibility; therefore it is easier for parents and caregivers to shield their child, for a short time at least, from realizing their difference from their peers. This opportunity for 'passing', however, is usually temporary, and can arguably present more problems than it solves. The moment when the glass shatters, so to speak, and an individual suddenly becomes aware of their difference may be even more psychologically harmful for the child who has been sheltered from an understanding of such difference.

This potential danger was brought into sharp focus for me when using a childcare provider for additional support needs. As I have mentioned before, with my son unable to attend 'mainstream' childcare this provider was a lifeline. However, this was not without a price. I was at once relieved for the help, and devastated that we needed it. I was able to reconcile this internal turmoil with the knowledge that he enjoyed his days there, that he too was benefiting from the service. One day, however, several weeks into his time with them, Micah returned home troubled. 'Those other children aren't like me, Mama. Why am I there?' he asked.

While he loved the activities and the staff, he could not reconcile his own identity with that of the other children there. He, to all intents and purposes, 'passed' as 'normal'. His discomfort at being confronted with the reality that he in fact might share something in common with children whose impairments were, admittedly, much more profound was palpable. Balancing his need to feel 'normal' against my own need for support, I consequently gave up the brief respite this service had afforded us both. This decision, ultimately, was formed out of stigma – both our own, and our awareness of others' stigma. While we were, in our own way, 'othered', we were also complicit in 'othering' his peers who could not so easily conceal their difference. Our discomfort functioned to our own detriment, and was a harsh and valuable lesson in humility.

This anecdote raises another particular difficulty with childhood disabilities: the question of disclosure. For children with impairments, disclosure is a significant challenge and one that is perhaps unique to the experience of children. I remember being called to a multi-agency meeting with the purpose of discussing the 'disclosure' of his autism to him. I myself had only recently learned of his diagnosis, and had ferociously thrown myself into researching and adapting. What I had not considered, however, was that Micah's own awareness of his condition would be so problematic.

I was strongly advised to wait until he was older to reveal his diagnosis to him; in the first instance this was in respect of his potential ability to comprehend it and, in the second, of its potential damage to his sense of self in relation to others. This was perplexing to me. While these justifications made complete sense and I, as a neutral observer, agree with them in the abstract, as Micah's mother the question of not telling him who he is seemed counter-intuitive. Scarlet felt similarly, reflecting, 'I know there's this big debate on whether or not to tell your child but it never occurred to me not to tell her.' Scarlet raised the important point that, for her, disclosing to her child was crucial to being able to explain her involvement with so many medical professionals, and also for her to be able to gain a sense of understanding herself. Abigail echoed this sentiment, although her particular situation was complicated by her daughter, in being over the age of 12, having to give consent for her own diagnostic process. She stressed however that, for her, telling her children was never in question.

For my part, the dilemma over whether or not to disclose would prove to be irrelevant; Micah, characteristically, figured it out on his own. In 2016, the National Autistic Society released a video entitled 'TMI', depicting a young boy with autism experiencing sensory overload during a shopping trip. Described as a virtual reality experience for neurotypical individuals to understand the challenges faced by those with autism, the short video immersed the viewer in an onslaught of competing noises that gradually increase in volume, along with the young boy's clearly distressed breathing. This video, it would seem, so accurately portrayed the experience that it prompted my son, who at such a time was unaware of his diagnosis, to ask, 'Mum, do I have autism? That's what I feel like!'

For adults, there is rarely a question of how or if they should be informed of their impairment, but for children their knowledge and understanding of their own condition is often largely dependent on adults. Perhaps reflective of this inter-dependency, children in disability studies are rarely discussed in isolation of their relational ties to adults. With some considering this relationality as further functioning to oppress the lives of disabled children, there is an increasing call for disability studies, and indeed practitioners and educators, to consider the voice of the children themselves. Emerging bodies of literature suggest that children's agency in articulating their own experience and contributing to their own support is crucial to their equal status as social beings (Mallett and Runswick-Cole, 2010). Undoubtedly, further study is required to explore the experience of children with disabilities from their own perspective, particularly as this subject raises significant ethical challenges in respect to the capacity, susceptibility and reliability of children in making informed decisions on important subjects such as healthcare (Prout and Hallett, 2003, p. 1).

However, studies have shown that society's disablement of children extends to the family, in respect to employment opportunities, access to resources and support, and the social lives of caregivers (Dowling and Dolan, 2001, p. 23). In Chapter 2, I outlined the complexity of autism symptoms, developing a picture of the lived experience of these challenges that demonstrated that often the symptoms of sensory sensitivity and difficulties in social relations combine to produce an autistic experience in which participation and inclusion in dominant social structures and settings can be particularly problematic. Writing of his son, Brian Brock provocatively proclaims, 'Adam has disabled me.' While on the surface this is a jarring admission, he goes on to clarify that, 'To say Adam has disabled me is ultimately to draw attention to the hard work that goes into mediating between him and his limits and capacities as he negotiates a world in which it is assumed that he lacks the basic capacities of normal citizens' (Brock, 2019, p. 7).

This mediation, in my experience, is multi-layered. There is the mediation between professionals: doctors, psychologists, education and social work. Then there is the mediation between the world as we perceive it, and the world as children with autism experience it. While I admittedly will never – can never – know what it is like to be Micah, being in his world and learning to predict, navigate and, in some cases, avoid the myriad of environmental triggers that he might find 'disabling' has similarly 'disabled' me. After so many years, even when Micah is not with me, I remain hyper-alert to noise levels, to busyness, to unexpected changes of plan. In this sense, his way of being in the world has similarly changed mine. In being 'in his world', I have also sadly learned that we are often 'outsiders' to the social worlds of others.

David Gray observes in his article on stigma perception that in addition to the individual with autism facing stigma, families also experience stigma as a consequence of their relationship to the stigmatized individual – in this case, their child (Gray, 1997, p. 103). This research is consistent with what Goffman refers to as the phenomenon of 'courtesy stigma'. 'Stigma perception', or the intense awareness of others and their potentially negative opinions of both the child and the parent, is considered to significantly affect not only maternal well-being, but also the likelihood of participating in leisure activities outside the home, attending social events, and seeking social support (Duerte et al., 2005, p. 417).

This may be a particularly relevant and interesting area of further study in relating to parenting as a unique experience of courtesy stigma, as parents arguably experience stigma both in terms of their relationship to the child, and also, as we have learned from Kanner, in terms of their perceived responsibility concerning the behaviours their child displays. As such, the experience of disabled children is intricately, and arguably inextricably, bound up with the experience of their caregivers. This interdependency impacts not only on how the impaired child is socially valued, but also on those who care for them. In the following chapter, I will explore how the complexity of this 'interdependent' stigma is lived and experienced, reflecting on how the 'gazes' of others can function to make our 'invisible' lives feel uncomfortably visible.

10

Averted Gazes: Living with Stigma

In previous chapters, I have discussed how the particular paradox of autism being a condition that is physically invisible, but whose symptoms manifest in deeply stigmatizing social behaviours, makes it a distinctly challenging experience. Stigma perception associated with autism is a particularly challenging issue as autism is, by its very nature, an 'invisible disability'. Therefore, the social recognition or empathy potentially evoked by a visible disability does not occur in autism. In reflecting on this, this chapter explores 'stigma' as one of the most profoundly impactful sources of marginalization and oppression on autistic lives, and those of their caregivers.

In earlier sections, I have highlighted that although autism does not have any outward physical markers, it is very difficult for individuals on the spectrum to 'conceal' their behaviour. Thus we have individuals with 'normal' appearances who are behaving 'abnormally'. This may be arguably more stigmatizing for individuals on the spectrum, who may face doubt as to the validity of their condition by virtue of their appearance. Tom Reynolds, in his introduction to *Vulnerable Communion: A Theology of Disability and Hospitality*, laments 'I cannot count the number of times friends and acquaintances of ours have exclaimed "but he seems so normal!" In fact, this has been a source of great pain. For Chris cannot live under the weight of these expectations' (Reynolds, 2008, p. 12). In disclosing Micah's condition to others, I too have lost count of the times I have been told, 'Oh ... well, you couldn't tell. He's very normal'. In my weaker moments I have received this as assurance that we were successfully 'passing'. In my stronger moments, I have been incensed by the unconscious stigma such a 'well meaning' comment conveys.

The ambiguity and misunderstandings of autism as a diagnostic category can be seen to shape attitudes towards it. The characteristics associated with an early indication of autism are often behavioural, which – when seen in a positive light – may be considered merely a 'quirk of personality' that can be moderated with a bit of self-control. In other cases, particularly when the child is less profoundly affected by autism, they may simply be regarded as strange or unlikeable (Macaskill, 2019, p. 29). For both Clara Claiborne Park and Jenny Lexhed, the schism between 'normal' appearance and 'abnormal' behaviour tainted both their own perceptions of autism, and how they feared they would be perceived by others:

> For Carl and me, autism has a stigma. It feels abstract, scary, and awful. We didn't know much about it, and we have preconceived notions – that autistics are mentally retarded people who cannot speak, and sit and rock in a corner, doomed to live in their own isolated world. That was what we envisioned when we first heard the word 'autism'. (Lexhed, 2015, p. 49)

Clara Claiborne Park admitted her own terror that others might look at her daughter with barely concealed horror as a consequence of her habit of mumbling:

> Because there can't be mumbles. There mustn't be. I remember the middle-aged woman I encountered in a bus station, mumbling under her breath to nobody at all – the frisson I felt, of pity but also fear. Jessy was still young; my imagination leapt ahead. Would she be like that, grown too old to be charming, still mumbling? If I felt fear, what could I expect from others? (Claiborne Park, 2002, p. 60)

Sadly, what we can expect from others is often a reinforcement of our fears. In his introduction to *Vulnerable Communion: A Theology of Disability and Hospitality*, Tom Reynolds reflects on receiving a call from his minister, who reluctantly informed him that the other parents of the parish did not want his son to return to Sunday school. The 'diagnostic indicators' described in Chapter 2 may often translate into child behaviours that are difficult for others to deal with. For Reynolds, his child's behaviours ranged from 'profanity, a lack of sensitivity to other children's personal space ... and an unpredictably violent imagination when playing with toys' (Reynolds, 2008, p. 11). Such behaviours presented an uncomfortable threat to the other members of the congregation, who 'did not want their children exposed to this child and feared what he represented'.

While David Gray noted that parents of children with more aggressive characteristics were considerably more likely to experience such stigma than children whose behaviours were 'passive' (Gray, 1993, 1997), even 'passive' autistic characteristics – such as stimming, rocking, humming or, in my son's case, unusual interests – can be shown to attract negative attention. Abigail reflected that even the resources and tools she employed to manage her children's anxiety so that meltdowns were less frequent – for example, ear defenders, Theraputty and other stimulatory toys – also attracted negative attention. Abigail recalled that even when her son was able to manage his 'unseemly' behaviours during Mass, the methods he used to help mitigate his sensory anxiety in the busyness of church still drew stares: 'There's many a time when we've been to church and there's been judgemental looks.'

Brian Brock, speaking of his experience as father to a boy with both Down's syndrome and autism, speaks of what he terms 'averted gazes' within the church and of his experience of 'courtesy stigma' at witnessing the discomfort, annoyance and discomfort of those in his congregation towards the son he 'gazes at in love' (Brock, 2019, p. 6). Such gazes of judgement and discomfort can therefore not only be seen to fall on the children themselves, but also on the parents who are perceived to be responsible for them. Consequently, we are very often considered to be 'bad parents' of 'bad children'.

Scarlet felt strongly that the behaviours associated with her daughter were often inextricably linked by others to her own perceived failings as a mother. 'Bad parenting,' she commented. 'I still get "done" with bad parenting.' I expressed to Naomi my own reluctance to engage with other parents at the school gates or admit to staff when we were struggling, certain that what they had witnessed would be a cause for judgement. Naomi described her own encounter with another mother at the school gates, which merely reinforced my fears:

> It's the hiddenness of autism that's difficult ... the way he acts sometimes in public ... I just let him get on with it, but you do feel people staring.
>
> I even had one mum say to me I would love your life; you just swan about and do what you do and I'm like *really*? You have no idea that I haven't slept for two days and he's running out of school, sitting for two hours in the boot of a car trying to talk him into school.

All of us were able to reflect on incidents in which we were ostracized or excluded from some form of social situation: birthday parties, school discos, after-school clubs. Sometimes the stigma was covert, concealed by 'forgotten invitations', but it was on occasions overt – being asked to 'deal with' our child, asked to leave, or being openly remarked upon were sadly not uncommon situations.

I recently had a conversation with someone in my family about one particular Christmas in which an extended family member came with their new partner. I remember being anxious that the busyness and excitement of the holiday would overwhelm my son, and that he would not be able to cope. Christmas was always a challenging day for us, the over-stimulation almost inevitably resulted in agitation, aggression or exhaustion. To my surprise and delight, he was excited and eager to tell everyone about his presents. That year his special interest was geology, and so he received a collection of gemstones and fossils that he was particularly keen to show off to his cousins. I was incredibly proud, and admittedly relieved, by the lovely memory he created for us all that day.

I later learned that following our departure, the guest of my relative remarked, 'What a strange child. What kind of nine-year-old wants a bunch of rocks for Christmas? He's very weird, isn't he?' In the case of our Christmas guest, they expected my son's behaviour to match his appearance – a nine-year-old boy that they presumed would be into cars or football. Upon being told of my son's condition, they brusquely replied, 'Well, that explains it. I knew he wasn't normal.' I had been used to stigma at the school gates, in the supermarket, at play parks. After so many years, I was steeled to the stares of strangers. This particular judgement, in a place where we felt safe and loved, came as an unexpected blow – in part because I had been so proud of his ability to have, at least what I perceived to be, a 'normal' Christmas Day for the first time. I was at once furious and devastated that she had taken this achievement away from him ... But yet there remained the nagging doubt, had I merely been lying to myself about how others see him?

Perhaps the most insidious part of stigma in this regard is that it is cyclical. It turns the gaze inwards, leading the gazed-upon person feeling exposed and full of self-doubt, and at the same time turns the gaze back on the gazer, leaving the judger, judged. I am somewhat ashamed to admit that this particular moment of stigmatization reproduced this same stigma in me; despite my best efforts, that one moment has coloured how I have perceived this person ever since. How, then, is such a cycle broken?

For the most part, the mothers I spoke with said that they dealt with stigma by developing a 'thick skin' to the stares of others, steeling themselves for judgement. At other times, stigma was actively resisted by challenging people's negative attitudes, and attempting to educate them on our children's condition. Shortly after my son's diagnosis, I remember buying small cards that described autism so that I could give them to people who showed strong reactions to his behaviour. Abigail observed that 'sunflower' lanyards were particularly helpful for her children in subtly indicating to others that they had an invisible condition. Naomi commented that, for her, providing others with the knowledge demanded greater sensitivity from them:

I'm more vocal since his diagnosis ... I have no shame in telling someone that he does have Asperger's, or if he's going somewhere he does need to have an adult because he does need one-to-one support. We don't have to tell people why, but I think no, why should we pretend that he doesn't. I'm a believer that if the children are aware of what he's got and they understand, then if they put him in a situation where he has a meltdown, they're complicit in that and they can't get away with it. I don't let people put him in that position easily.

Scarlet and Abigail both noted, however, that education does not always correlate with greater understanding. Both described engagements with healthcare professionals who, despite being assumed to 'know better', displayed the very attitudes they were expected to dispel. Describing her daughter's diagnostic process, Abigail commented that one particular professional remarked, 'She's just doing this to wind her mother up ... If she has autism, I'll eat my hat.' Scarlet reflected on a similar conversation with her daughter's educational psychologist:

She said, 'I'm begging you please not to label her, if you push for a diagnosis she'll be held back and stigmatized in school and she's so clever ... if you do this you'll cause her to miss out.'
And I thought, you're a professional! In my head I'm thinking I've worked with a lot of special needs children, and it really upsets me when people look at it as a stigma and a label. The only reason it could be is that people make it that way.

These reflections suggest that an inherent difficulty is that stigma is not only experienced socially, but also institutionally: which has significantly more far-reaching consequences in respect to diagnosis and support. Scarlet raises a particularly intriguing issue: that stigma can often be a self-fulfilling prophecy. She questioned whether the professional in her daughter's case was in fact perpetuating stigma by the mere fact of anticipating it. Burack and colleagues raised similar queries in respect to the reciprocity that takes place in the context of autism. He suggests that, by their very differences, people with autism produce different social responses in others, thus inadvertently shaping their social experience:

> ... children with autism, therefore, experience a distinctly different social world than that experienced by other children from a very early age, as their unusual behaviour affords different sorts of interactions from those that other children usually experience. Not only do they experience or understand the world differently from other children, their world really is different from that of other children, simply because they are in it. (Burack et al., 2001, p. 27)

II

Disabled Bodies, Able World?

Despite the fact that, as we have seen, impairment had (and arguably continues to have) profound and far-reaching social consequences for the disabled individual, the relationship between the social body and the impaired one was not considered until the late 1960s and early 1970s. Influenced by the critical lens of theorists such as Michel Foucault, 1970s Britain witnessed an emerging movement that challenged how we consider disability, and what this meant for disabled lives. Proponents of the social model – most notably disability theorists such as Mike Oliver and Paul Abberley – contended that the most debilitating effects of disablement were not symptoms of impairment, but rather social attitudes.

The infantilization of physically disabled individuals (sometimes referred to as the 'personal tragedy model'), they argued, consigned the impaired individual to the role of victim, preserving disability as something unfortunate, pitiable and reliant. The assumption that physical impairment naturally implied mental impairment strongly influenced public policy, with political, civil and sexual rights paternalized by the state (Campbell and Oliver, 1996, p. 28). Further to the social barriers they perceived were constructed to exclude individuals with impairments, disability theorists also challenged the perspective that bodily impairments limited mobility. Rather, they argued, participation in work and leisure activities were inhibited by inaccessible buildings, poor public transport links, and public spaces that were designed purely for the able-bodied.

The Union of the Physically Impaired Against Segregation (UPIAS), comprised of individuals who were themselves disabled, proposed that in contrast to the medical model that considers disability to be causally linked to impairment, disability is in fact the consequence of a disabling environment – one that creates social, spatial and financial barriers to impaired individuals leading full and inclusive social lives (Oliver, 2002, p. 12).

Recent decades have witnessed a dramatic shift from the paternalistic model of welfare towards policies that centre around inclusivity and equal access to all areas of public life. Though arguably hard won, the social model can be seen to have had some success in contributing towards these shifting attitudes towards disability. The World Health Organization's ICIDH schema (International Classification of Impairments, Disabilities and Handicaps) has altered its definition of disability, reflecting the importance of changing the language we use to describe disability:

> The term 'disability' has been replaced with 'disablement', with a focus on limits to activities, and 'handicap' is superseded by considerations of participation; impairment remains as before – loss or abnormality of psychological, physiological or anatomical structure or function. (Thomas, 2002, p. 42)

In 2013, the Scottish government introduced 'Keys to Life', a policy strategy influenced by the UN Convention of Rights and adopted by both public and private social care organizations. This strategy is designed to promote a commitment to ensuring individuals with physical or learning disabilities have equal access to healthcare, education and housing, and are supported to have choice, control and independence in their lives as active, fully recognized citizens. The divide between 'mainstream' and 'special' education is becoming increasingly permeable, with local authorities encouraged to make learning adaptations rather than separations. Such changes mark a dramatic turn in history from the situation for individuals with disabilities a century ago. The social and structural barriers designed to conceal, marginalize and victimize individuals with impairments have gradually begun to be dismantled.

This shift in consciousness away from disablement being something inherently flawed and inescapable in the individual, to being something external and socially constructed, was transformative for many impaired individuals. Carol Thomas observes that 'when disabled individuals encounter the social model, the effect is often revelatory and liberatory; enabling them, perhaps for the first time, to recognize most of their difficulty as socially caused' (Thomas, 2002, pp. 38–40). Proponents of the social model and organizations such as UPIAS have reframed disability as a form of social oppression, speaking of 'disablism' in the same context as 'racism' and 'sexism'. In considering themselves as an oppressed group rather than victims of personal circumstance, disabled individuals are able to assert some agency over how they consider their impairment.

While some adopted the ethos of the social model at solely the individual level, utilizing it as a tool to alter their self-perception and outlook from a 'disabled person' to an 'individual with impairments', the social model also operated at the socio-political level, applying pressure for legislative changes. This was not a simple undertaking. If we are to assume, as the social model proposes, that society, rather than the individual, is the problem for those with disabilities, we are left with the huge problem of changing society.

From deviant bodies to liberated souls?

In upholding a social minority perspective of disability, liberation theologies of disability draw on the themes above to assert that theology has a problematic relationship with disability in a number of respects. The first, at a fundamentally practical level, is that religious institutions can be a particularly inaccessible place for individuals with disabilities, both physically and organizationally (Macaskill, 2019, p. 41). The second is that disability has been pathologized, particularly within the Christian tradition. It is often represented through 'personal tragedy models of disability' in which bodily difference is considered to be something that defines an individual as 'lesser', 'other' or not 'whole' in their personhood (Eiesland, 1994, p. 92). Third, these factors often coalesce into stigmatizing attitudes to inclusion that (consciously or unconsciously) treat persons with disabilities as inferior or incapable (Swinton, 2012a, p. 444). As a consequence, disabled experience is not represented, and disabled voices are often silenced within theological contexts. Naming the absence of attention to the spiritual dimensions of people's lives within contemporary disability studies (Creamer, 2009, p. 78), liberation theologies of disability traverse the disciplinary boundaries between disability studies and theology.

A synthesis of Christian theology and socio-economic inquiry, liberation theologies came to prominence in the second half of the twentieth century, predominantly within a Roman Catholic Latin American context (Streck, 2012, p. 526). Influenced by Catholic social teaching's 'preferential option for the poor', theologians such as Gustavo Gutiérrez (1973) and Leonardo Boff (1986) proposed a shift to liberation theologies in response to issues of poverty and social injustice (Streck, 2012, p. 527). This response has since been enthusiastically embraced in increasingly wider contexts (such as feminism and post-colonialism) as a form of theological thinking that particularly speaks to issues of oppression and marginalization. In doing so, they position themselves as sites of resistance against structures of inequality (Eiesland, 1994, p. 28). Strongly influenced by the social model movement, liberation theologies similarly view disability as being a socially constructed discourse and shaped by political and economic dimensions (Eiesland, 1994, p. 13; Betcher, 2007, p. 11).

Liberation theologies of disability are often developed from the standpoint of an 'insider perspective' by those who occupy a body that, in one respect or another, has been defined as 'different'. Drawing upon key emphases in disability studies, central concerns include issues of social recognition, accessibility and inclusion. In challenging the lack of representation of disabled experience, such perspectives have offered an alternative theology that speaks to disabled individuals' own lived experience. We have been challenged to imagine a God with

Down's syndrome (Swinton, 2003), a God who is blind (Hull, 2001) and a God who is 'crippled' (Eiesland, 1994). Such representations aim to oppose the particular inaccessibility of religious symbols (for example, 'wholeness') for disabled bodies, asserting the position that, 'If God is disabled, then exclusive and excluding practices cannot be tolerated' (Swinton, 2012a, p. 446). Providing a re-imagining of the symbolic tradition that she considers has been historically misappropriated to the detriment of disabled lives, Nancy Eiesland proposes:

> ... that a liberatory theology of disability must create new images of wholeness as well as new discourses. Furthermore, the bodily rituals of stigmatization and exclusion that are a significant form of oppression of people with disabilities must be supplanted by bodily practices of ordinary inclusion. (Eiesland, 1994, p. 92)

Eiesland here can be seen to echo feminist disability theorist Liz Crow in asserting that a recognition of the impaired body does not diminish the socio-cultural dimensions of oppression imposed on it (Crow, 1996, p. 3). It is worth noting, though, that many of the theological perspectives explored above are put forward by individuals who are not traditional members of the 'theological guild'. Both Eiesland and Block share a sociological background in disability studies, with an interest in the religious lives of the disabled (Creamer, 2009, p. 88). Their interdisciplinary approach arguably reinforces the lack of attention given to disability from within theology itself. While their 'theological credibility' may be challenged as a consequence of this, I propose rather that in occupying these 'insider'/'outside' positions, such perspectives are in fact well placed to generate theological thinking outside of the constraints of dominant theoretical frameworks (Goto, 2018, p. 32).

Swinton, however, while acknowledging the socio-political dimensions of disability, is uneasy about the way in which theology might become too comfortable in merely responding to social issues. In contrast to Betcher, he considers that:

... very often the conversation between social analysis and theology tends to move only one way: from the experience of disability toward changes in theology ... theology simply responds to the insights of sociology. There is no clear theological voice which can effectively challenge the sociological analysis. The premises are set before the conversation begins. (Betcher, 2007, p. 445)

This work, in articulating a social problem requiring a theological response, could be subjected to this critique. I also come from an interdisciplinary background, and while I respect Swinton's conviction that theology should develop its own voice, I suggest that his perspective assumes a theological history that neglects the reality of our lived experience. Neither our lives, nor indeed our theological thinking, develop in a social/historical vacuum. Rather, as I have already articulated, our social histories profoundly affect our 'social presents'. Furthermore, this approach neglects the fact that a 'social analysis' of disabilities developed in such theological positions does not merely stem from a sociological interest, but from the real-life experiences of individuals whose lives have been touched by the very issues they seek to challenge.

However, despite my reservations, I do share another of Swinton's concerns in respect of who exactly counts as disabled in such theologies of disability (Swinton, 2012c, p. 175). While I acknowledge the usefulness of liberation theologies of disability in articulating the interplay between socio-political approaches and disabled lives that I have sought to identify in Chapters 1 and 2, I do so with an awareness that such theologies are themselves often shaped by the same dominant assumptions they seek to challenge.

In many ways, the social model can be seen to be the antithesis of the medical model in which disability is considered consequential to impairment. The social model introduced a radical way of considering disability, bringing into focus the social inequalities that have constrained the lives of disabled individuals. This focus, though, has been criticized for overshadowing what is arguably the *starting point* for the question of disability rights – that of the disabled person (Hughes, Goodley and Davis, 2012, p. 59). While liberatory on the one hand, the social model's rallying call against 'disabling social forces' relegated the impact of bodily impairment to the sidelines, considering that disability could be largely 'overcome' with equal access to public spaces, education and employment.

The Chair of Disability Studies at the University of Glasgow, Nick Watson, and sociologist Tom Shakespeare suggest that as admirable as the goal of adaptation may be, the claims of the early social model theorists can arguably be seen to be somewhat blurred by their own philosophical position. UPIAS in particular has been criticized as comprising a very narrow representation of disabled experience – composed largely of white, heterosexual men with predominantly physical impairments (often the result of accident or injury). Shakespeare and Watson propose that such organizations lacked the diversity and breadth of experience to give a more nuanced understanding of disabled lives (Shakespeare and Watson, 2010, p. 58). Furthermore, the social model's premise of 'adaptation' can be seen to be more concerned with adjustments to accommodate physical disabilities or sensory impairments such as blindness, while the experience of individuals with learning disabilities – which are arguably more social in both presentation and in effect – is largely absent. Shakespeare and Watson issue this challenge:

> What would it mean to create a barrier-free Utopia for people with learning difficulties? ... What about people on the autistic spectrum, who may find social contact difficult to cope with: a barrier-free Utopia might be a place where they did not have to meet, communicate with, or have to interpret other people ... Barrier-free enclaves are possible, but not a barrier-free world. (Shakespeare and Watson, 2010, p. 63)

As articulated above, the experience of disability for individuals with learning difficulties is often profoundly social, and arguably also profoundly different in many respects to individuals with solely physical impairments. With such different ranges of lived experience, can we assume that by mere juxtaposition to the 'normal' social body that their experiences of disability are the same? It is precisely this question that underpins much of the criticism levelled at the social model. To what extent does it acknowledge lived experience, and can there really be seen to be a universal lived experience of disability that can be reduced to one single group of those oppressed socially?

If disability is social, then impairment is bodily, and as such remains within the remit of medicine. Thus, in attempting to move past disability being defined by the body, towards a model in which disability is the shared experience of inequality, critics suggest that the social model *preserves* the biomedical discourse it seeks to supersede. Mike Bury proposes that the social model treats the disabled body as a taken-for-granted assumption, when in fact it is the body that is the site on which our reality becomes perceptible, particularly in relation to chronic conditions (Bury, 2010, p. 75). That disabled experience is shaped by bodily experience seems too obvious to ignore, and yet a narrative of impairment is often conspicuously absent from the social model.

Asserting the moral obligation of Christian communities to challenge the social oppression of individuals with disabilities, liberation theologies of disability are particularly concerned with issues of access, challenging the Church to make their structures and organizations more physically and intellectually inclusive spaces (Block, 2002, p. 21). However, as I showed in Chapter 1, notions of accessibility are typically based upon physical definitions of disability, evoking images of ramps, lifts, etc. Obviously, this is inherently problematic when considering the experience of autism.

In the context of the Church, the busyness of the environment and competing voices (in differing tones and registers) come together to present a significant sensory challenge for individuals with autism. Speaking of his own experience as a member of the Church who is also on the autism spectrum, Grant Macaskill maintains that churches could introduce many simple adaptations to improve the experience for individuals who find them inhospitable. The fact that churches are often slow to do so, he argues, demonstrates that practical problems of accessibility and inclusion can arguably be seen to be secondary to the Church's attitudes towards difference (Macaskill, 2019, p. 41).

The theologies of accessibility articulated above propose a model of inclusion that, while promoting an acceptance of bodily difference, assume a universality in respect to intellectual capacity that neglects cognitive developmental conditions such as autism (Swinton, 2012c, p. 177). Given that autism is characterized by difficulties in engaging in the social world that those without autism take for granted, it is perhaps naïve to believe we can make the social world accessible for people with autism in the same way that we can make buildings accessible.

In moving beyond the issue of accessibility, disability theorists such as Sharon Betcher propose a theology that asserts that genuine inclusion may only be attained by changing the way in which people are educated and socialized to value one another through a radical change in attitudes. However, Brian Brock counters the assumption that such solutions can ever address the challenges that disability raises, asserting that 'all the ramps and lifts in the world are a poor substitute for open hearts' (Brock, 2019, p. 2). Social attitudes, he shrewdly points out, are much harder to adapt.

The same room, a different year. A different Micah. This was our third multi-agency review, and perhaps the hardest one yet. In all of his previous meetings, referrals and appointments, I had my mother by my side, his staunch defender; 'the Micah whisperer', I called her. She had left us four weeks earlier, finally succumbing to what had been a ferocious and determined battle with cancer. Before her passing, life with Micah had plateaued into a grinding, anxious, relentless struggle. All of the carefully negotiated strategies we had implemented at home, the stability of consistent routines, the ability to anticipate the next day's challenges by making sure the RIGHT jumper was clean ... all of those had been thrown into disarray by the emergent necessity of my mother's palliative care. Gone were our Tuesday and Sunday night dinners, gone were his Friday sleepovers. Gone too was his mother, who was now shuffling hollowly through his days, struggling to maintain the façade that things were, or ever could be, normal.

The door opened and a stranger burst in, visibly harassed. I don't remember much of the minutes before that, other than staring blankly at the table unable to meet the sympathy in the eyes sitting around me. This unexpected arrival cracked the defence of my numbness. 'Duty Social Work. Apologies for the delay, Micah hasn't been re-allocated a social worker yet, so I was asked to attend at the last minute. Where are we at?' The stranger was keen to get straight to the point and avoid being late for his next appointment. The chair cleared her throat. 'Well, we didn't know you were attending ... but it's very good of you to come. I'm not sure if you are aware but Eilidh has just experienced a significant bereavement, and a great loss of support to both her and Micah, so it would be of benefit to them both to have some input from your department.' He nodded at her, turning to me. 'So, what can we do for you?'

'I ... I don't know. We'd only just met a social worker, and she took Micah out to soft play so that I could look after Mum or just get a break; she brought her dog to visit him when he was sad ... we were just getting to know each other when she left so we hadn't completed his needs assessment yet...' I pause, aware that he is expecting me to provide something concrete, tangible, for him to respond to. 'Our needs are ... mornings are probably the hardest, he really struggles with dressing ... and I'm missing a lot of work because he can't always manage the school day, I'm always being called away because he needs me ... We had a night once a week that my mum would take him, so that we both got some space from each other, and I could work or get some rest ... I don't know what Social Work do ... or can do ... but I just ... we don't really have any support now.'

The stranger looked exasperated, abruptly shutting his notebook. 'I'm very sorry for your loss, Miss Campbell. But if you don't actually know what you want, I'm really not sure how we can help you. It sounds to me, to be frank, like you need a babysitter. That's not something the local authority can provide. You have our number if you're really struggling but, in the meantime, perhaps it's best for us to withdraw until your needs become clearer.' With that, he excused himself, leaving a room of shocked expressions. It was to be ten months before Micah was assigned another social worker. Months of desperately trying to soothe the grief of a child who doesn't understand what grief is, just that he is angry, and sad, and I am not his nanny.

12

Struggling for Support

With the estimated national cost for individuals with ASD (Autism Spectrum Disorders) estimated at £2.292 billion per annum, and financial costs to families estimated to be between £3,813 and £4,479 per annum, the importance of providing timely and appropriate support to individuals and families affected by autism has very real material implications for public policy in Scotland.[1] Given the breadth and pervasiveness of autism symptoms, successful strategies for autism support are expected to traverse health, education and social welfare policy. However, such policies are inevitably subject to budget constraints, and sadly the needs of the minority often do not factor into the needs of the social majority. Gillibrand writes, 'often the struggle comes down to micro politics, to the unending battle of individual carers to make the system work for those for whom they care' (Gillibrand, 2009, p. 170).

Between the meeting I have described above, and our eventual reallocation of a social worker, was a gap of ten months. During this time, I called, wrote to, pleaded with – and ultimately berated – our local authority to re-engage with us. Eventually, after the intervention of a local MSP (Member of Scottish Parliament), we received a reallocation, a support worker and a formal apology from the department. While we eventually got the support that we so desperately needed, the amount of time spent advocating for my son – time that could have been spent with him – weighed heavily on me. I was not alone in feeling that the attempts to advocate for support were often equally as stressful as the circumstances for which we needed support. Abigail discussed similar experiences of struggling against institutional barriers, facing many denials and refusals in the diagnostic process as a consequence of being dismissed as a mother merely exaggerating the challenges of parenting:

> We've had a long fight ... I'm probably not particularly well liked within the local authority because I had to push for my son to get into his school, but I felt it was my duty to get him the outcome he deserved.

Scarlet repeatedly echoed this imagery of 'fighting', often describing herself as 'battling', 'being up against a brick wall' and 'banging her head against the wall'. The use of such metaphors illuminates the fact that mothers of children with autism are often forced to undertake a very different role to 'caregiver'; they are often required to fight and advocate for their child's healthcare, education and inclusion against a culture that does not take seriously their experience. We were just as, if not more, affected by the responses to autism from employers, family members, schools and professionals as we were from our child's symptoms. In reflecting upon both my own and my participants' experiences of struggle, they were rooted in the frustratingly unremarkable activities and routines of our everyday lives, but also battles waged at a much larger social and institutional level.

For Scarlet, while her daughter's symptoms were in and of themselves a significant source of difficulty, her struggle was made harder by social attitudes and barriers to diagnosis that challenged and trivialized her experience:

> So they tested her and in their words ... and this is something that has been a source of frustration with me for some years with my daughter ... as far as the professionals are concerned, they tested her on all these various academic areas, maths, literacy, etc., and she tested at the highest range for all these areas, so therefore, in their words, there couldn't possibly be anything 'wrong with her'.
>
> And I have an issue with that 'Nothing wrong with them' ... because either way there's nothing 'wrong' with them,

but just because someone excels academically doesn't mean they're not having these other issues, doesn't mean they're not crying themselves to sleep or having these other emotional issues ... the doctors say there's nothing wrong with her and again it was really, really frustrating for me ...

She was being excluded from school every other day, I was getting the phone call and having to come down, she'd be excluded for a week. I would have to work out the childcare because I was a working parent, as well as being a single parent from when she was five years old. And I was banging my head against the wall trying to get somewhere.

Scarlet's experience reinforces some of the particular challenges autism presents for those advocating for support and understanding for their lived experience. As discussed in previous chapters, the invisibility of autism, coupled with the fact that it is a condition that presents itself most acutely in daily experiences such as sleeping, dressing, eating and social interactions, makes it all too easy for others to challenge the veracity of the struggles faced because they are often concealed within the home. In the opening reflection to this chapter, I have described how difficult it is for mothers to articulate the challenges and struggles we face, particularly when such struggles are often rooted in daily trials considered to be too mundane, too banal, too inconsequential, to justify the words 'challenges' and 'struggle', much less to be considered valid reasons to be given support.

Each of the women I spoke to discussed the strain of an ASD diagnosis on relationships; however, for many it was often other family members or those in their wider social circle who struggled to come to terms with a positive diagnosis, often preferring to deny the reality of the situation to the detriment of their own relationship with the child. Scarlet discussed that not presenting as 'autistic enough' can often lead to others raising doubts over her daughter's diagnosis, which can often feel like a lack of acceptance of who her daughter is and the struggles that they share:

My siblings feel the same way, my ex-husband doesn't ac-knowledge that there's an issue. And people who have known her for her entire life … even other children on the autism spectrum can be the same.

While Scarlet has been able to maintain relationships with those in her life who reject her daughter's diagnosis, this has often been the result of her developing a 'thick skin' to their opinions and abdicating her own right to turn to them for support. However, it is not always possible to maintain rela-tionships in the face of such rejections. Abigail spoke about the painful reality of her parents' refusal to accept her daughter's Asperger's:

It's torn my family apart. It's absolutely torn it apart. My son was somewhat easier to accept in some ways because so many of the signs were there so early. But my parents are quite old fashioned.

So far as my daughter is concerned, my parents were absolutely determined she wasn't on the spectrum, and if I even considered putting her forward for an assessment they wanted nothing to do with me. So, our whole family was torn apart last year, because I wanted my daughter assessed, my daughter agreed to it, and my parents forbade me from doing it. My parents also owned the house that I lived in, so we became homeless, because they decided that if I wasn't going their way, I was being cut off. That was the reality of it. They just can't accept my child's diagnosis at all.

For Abigail, her parents' denial was not merely a symptom of their processing of the new reality of their granddaughter's condition, but had very real, material consequences for the whole family. At a practical level, important sources of support are withdrawn leading to further stress and isolation for the parent or parents; at an emotional level, such a schism within the family can be devastating for all involved and is often diffi-cult to repair once broken. Kearney and Griffin observe that,

Whilst sorrow seems self-evident, a great deal of pain derives from societal values and beliefs mirrored in the words and behaviours of friends, family and professionals. In a better world, this pain could be avoided. On the other hand, existential pain and grief [Stephenson and Murphy, 1986] cannot be avoided, as it cannot be ameliorated by education and attitudinal change. (Kearney and Griffin, 2001, p. 588)

Hospitable communities?

In my personal reflection at the start of this chapter, I revealed that one's ability to cope with the challenges presented by autism often requires considerable social support, but that sadly such requests for support are frequently met inhospitably. Both Abigail and Vera described challenges in obtaining acceptance for their children's conditions from within their own families, highlighting that even when ties are perceived to be unconditional, they cannot always be counted upon to be so. Brock proposes that in this respect:

Conditions such as autism reveal communities. The appearance of disability brings to the surface the capacity of individuals and social networks to affirm and support those who present challenges with grace and genuine appreciation. (Brock, 2019, p. 29)

Communitarian theologies respond to Brock's challenge for attitudinal change by positioning the Church as being at the heart of a community that is responsive to, and responsible for, a compassionate bearing with one another's burdens. Influenced by the work of Karl Barth in responding to times of social crises and fragmentation, communitarian models advocate a return to Scripture as a means of providing coherence and constancy (Graham, Walton and Ward, 2018, p. 88). Informed by theologies that position the Bible as a means of providing the scripts that guide our actions, such an approach both reconstructs and reaffirms a coherent Christian identity that is not only rooted in faith but lived and enacted in acts shaped by uniquely Christian values (Hauerwas, 1990, p. 55).

Bringing together elements of liberation theologies that propose a commitment to challenging social injustice and marginalization, and principles of Catholic social teaching that engage in the practice of mutual solidarity and compassionate obligation to one another, communitarian disability theologies highlight the potential of disabled lives to unsettle and challenge our perceptions of what a community of genuine acceptance should look like (Brock, 2019, p. 137; Swinton, 2012c, p. 184). A communitarian model of disability must therefore foster the level of inclusion and acceptance that would significantly challenge the stigma, judgement and exclusion that I have shown colours the lives of mothers of children on the spectrum.

The work of influential theological ethicist Stanley Hauerwas is foundational to the communitarian model's response to issues of disability. In contrast to the liberation theologies outlined above, Hauerwas was particularly concerned to explore how the experience of individuals with cognitive and intellectual disabilities might shine a spotlight on our communal moral character – revealing how we value persons with difference (Hauerwas, 2005, p. 54). John Swinton, who develops the communitarian approach of Hauerwas, is also particularly concerned with how theology responds to intellectual conditions such as Down's syndrome (Swinton, 2003), autism (Swinton and Trevett, 2009; Swinton, 2012b) and dementia (Swinton, 2012d). He has been particularly vocal in critiquing theologies of accessibility as concealing the dynamics of power at play in excluding individuals with cognitive difference, which I have shown to be problematic in relation to autism. Naming the potential to misconstrue 'pity' as 'compassion', Swinton asserts that merely identifying as Christian does not inherently imbue individuals with the ability to offer genuine solidarity in the face of such perceived suffering (Swinton, 2003, p. 11). He cautions that,

> The Church can only truly call itself a community when it reveals inclusive love. It can only reveal inclusive love when it realises the limitations of its human-made boundaries, and

strives to build a space for love; a space in the midst of the complexities of theology and tradition; a space which is not dependent on a person's intellect for access; a space in which all persons can be enabled to be themselves in the company of others. (Swinton, 1997, p. 18)

Rather, he affirms the need for a Christian identity that is actively engaged in the faithful practice of Christian community (Swinton, 2012, p. 187). Swinton proposes that a genuinely hospitable Christian community begins with the recognition that God provides us with a blueprint for relationships formed out of equality, acceptance and love (Swinton, 2003, p. 69). In such a way, he is seeking a much deeper understanding of inclusion incarnated in committed communal life. In advocating unconditional acceptance over notions of accessibility, communitarian models of disability assert the revelatory potential of engaging in a caring relationship with another person without sympathy or expectation of reward (Nouwen, 1997, p. 43).

For Hauerwas, such a community can only be exemplified within the Church, although he suggests that the model for such a Church can be found in the micro-social location of families of individuals with intellectual or cognitive impairments. Hauerwas considered that parents of children with disabilities reveal a distinctly valuable and formative example of the kind of compassionate hospitality a Christian community is called to bestow. He proposes that the uncritical acceptance demonstrated by this parental model can offer a blueprint for the kind of patient, loving presence he believes to be critical in bearing sufferings that are ongoing, and from which no purpose or meaning can be drawn. He writes:

... caring for such children means more than simply providing them with the latest means of therapy or subjecting them to the current forms of educational or behaviour-modification theory. For care is not simply 'doing' things for these children, even when such 'doing' involves our best technologies, but it means knowing how to be with and regard these children with the respect they demand. (Hauerwas, 2005, p. 151)

Hauerwas's position affirms my assertion that the lived experience of parents affords significant potential in generating theological insights into disability generally, and autism in particular. In the first instance, it recognizes the argument I will further in Chapter 17 – that the knowledge of parents is a potential collaborative resource for professionals in both expediting diagnosis and in developing successful support strategies for children. Second, this position highlights that while parents are the primary source of care, they should not be the *only* source of care. I have proposed that attitudes that present parents – and in particular mothers – as being solely responsible for the development and behaviour of children place an undue burden of responsibility that functions to inhibit our ability to ask for support. This de-legitimizes the notion that any children – much less children with additional support needs – are the sole responsibility of the parents; this position reminds the Church of the real material implications and obligations of the promise offered in baptism (Hauerwas, 2005, p. 58).

Certainly, we mothers have all, at one time or another, considered how much lovelier life could be if others could demonstrate the same uncritical acceptance that we have developed for our children with autism. In being able to cope with the circuitous and often conflicting demands our mothering required, we all spoke of the importance, yet the struggle, of finding 'a tribe' we could rely on. While I was a 'single' mother for many years, I would not be truthful if I claimed to have raised Micah alone. Rather, a patchwork of teachers, friends and family members has formed a collective blanket of support around us.

Micah was fortunate enough to be in an exceptionally supportive primary school, where teachers approached his behaviours with patience, curiosity and acceptance. Indeed, some of those same teachers have become lifelong friends, if not 'family'. My mother, particularly, had an uncanny intuition when it came to Micah; she always knew exactly how to soothe him, or precisely when to challenge him. My father has delighted in facilitating Micah's obsessions, excitedly searching for new 'prizes' to add to his ever-evolving collections. My husband, for five straight years, scheduled his life around committing to seeing us every Tuesday, Thursday and Saturday, orienting his own needs around Micah's need for stability and routine. I have been graced with friends who have listened without judgement (and often with a very large glass of wine) on the days when I have admitted defeat.

John Gillibrand (2009), Tom Reynolds (2008) and Brian Brock (2019) have drawn on their own experiences as fathers to articulate the theological tension provoked by having a child with autism, reinforcing that attention to how someone orients their life around the needs of another can provide a deep and challenging theological reminder of our responsibility to welcome one another with compassionate hospitality (Reynolds, 2008, p. 42). Brian Brock admits that 'at the deepest level, and behind these more mundane hopes, I can hope to enjoy Adam. I hope that others, too will ... say with unfeigned sincerity: "I'm glad you're here"' (Brock, 2019, p. 193). Developing this position, Tom Reynolds considers that theologies that offer true inclusion must acknowledge that, rather than showing weakness, the vulnerability revealed by conditions such as autism highlights our mutual dependence, challenging us to find new ways of forming strong and loving connections with one another (Reynolds, 2008, p. 118).

All you need is love?

'Love', as I have sought to articulate, has been a problematic concept in cultural constructions of autism. By the very inclusion of 'abnormal reciprocal social action' as part of the diagnostic triad, the implication is clear – there is something fundamentally flawed in the relationship between autism and love. Yet there is also something peculiarly inherent in respect to love and autism; the condition is simultaneously presumed to be caused by a lack of love, and reciprocates this lack in its perceived ability to love another. Love, it would seem, poses a lot of questions in respect to autism.

John Swinton, however, proposes that it also offers the answers. Swinton himself considers 'love' to be a central and defining part of the human condition and, moreover, the Christian condition. Recognizing the tensions articulated above, he asks, how do individuals who are believed to struggle with expressing or interpreting emotions participate in supportive relationships, or indeed in religious traditions built on relationship with others? The answer to this question, Swinton believes, is not how those with autism love, but rather how we might come to 'think autistically' in self-critically examining our own normative constructions of abstract concepts such as 'love'. Swinton proposes that Christianity has become heavily influenced by Western cultural constructs of 'romantic love', which are often incompatible with images of individuals with autism as un-empathetic, undemonstrative and unfeeling.

In 'Reflections on autistic love' (2012b), Swinton looks to exactly these types of 'romantic' relationships to highlight that 'autistic love' does not demonstrate an absence of love, but rather provides a challenge to our perceptions of what love actually is. Rather than loving less strongly, Swinton aims to show that autistic people love differently. Referencing Christine Guth's article 'Horses Live to Run …', he describes the difficulty Christine experienced in coming to the revelation that for her autistic and 'unloving' husband, love was displayed in the seemingly inconsequential realities of daily routines; of tending to her garden, and his 'commitment to spending the last half-hour of every evening with me, reviewing the day'. Swinton proposes that:

> … to suggest that love for autistic people might mean something as apparently mundane as regularly digging the garden together is strangely dissonant. But that is the challenge that autistic love brings with it. Our old certainties are unsettled and newer, deeper truths become possible. (Swinton, 2012b, p. 277)

Rather than attempting to approach neurodiversity in terms of how it can be 'normalized' into traditional schemas of belief, Swinton advocates a seeing of 'thinking differently' as a generative and valuable gift to the Church. In reorienting our perception of difference away from a deficit model, he proposes that we are able to become a community which does not merely 'respond to' diversity but rather is enriched by it from within (Swinton, 2012b, p. 277). Here, we can see the strongly Hauerwasian influence of a perception of Christian community formed by uniquely Christian values:

> ... our understanding of love does not come from what we think love may or may not be but from that which is revealed of love by God in and through Christ. The nature of love is defined by the nature of God. Love is not a capacity, an experience or even a human possibility ... it is from this primal gift of love-in-Christ that all other manifestations of love take their shape and form. (Swinton, 2012b, p. 275)

Approaching this from a rare 'insider perspective' as a person with autism in the Church, Grant Macaskill draws on these ideas, together with Reynold's theological model of vulnerability, in appealing to a Pauline paradigm of human frailty that affirms the value of weakness and responds to it with love (Macaskill, 2019, p. 186). Drawing together the threads of acceptance and hospitality identified above, he considers that true acceptance of difference might require neurotypical individuals to sometimes adapt to the person with autism's way of being in and seeing the world, proposing a theology of 'accommodative love' (p. 118). A commitment to remembering and anticipating the minutiae of specific needs and wants a child with autism may have, whether that be – in Micah's case – the right socks, or as Naomi will go on to share, the correct yoghurt, demonstrates, I would argue, a model of loving attention that strongly resonates with Macaskill's model of 'accommodative love'. Arguably, it is this kind of adaptive love that enables mothers and caregivers to continue in the daily, and often seemingly insurmountable, challenges they face.

Such theological models of autism echo Brian Brock's position that inclusion does not necessarily mean 'accommodation', but rather a genuine and empathetic acceptance of difference (Brock, 2019, p. 2). This may have significant implications for the stigma of autistic characteristics that we have considered to be particularly problematic for both those on the spectrum and for their families. Proposing a response that attempts to bridge the experiential gap between the neurotypical person and the neuro-diverse person, without attempting to normalize or paternalize autistic difference, is particularly useful in considering how greater understanding and empathy may make our communities a less hostile and judgemental place for families with autism. However, Brock expresses his reluctance in presenting such models as being seen to be an attempt to 'think autistically' (Brock, 2019, p. 193).

I too share this reluctance. While I consider John Swinton's research to be insightful and challenging in proposing new models of theological thinking in respect to autism, I find his approach to be problematic for the particular research in this book in a number of respects. Although I support his contention that 'inclusion' can often in reality be better read as 'normalization', without a genuine and uncritical acceptance of difference, Swinton's own representations of autistic experience can arguably be seen to conform to the particular stereotypes he purports to be seeking to challenge. In 'Religion and autism' (Swinton and Trevett, 2009, p. 2), Swinton describes an individual who can only think in the black and white of literal language, for whom complex religious metaphors are confusing at best and frightening at worst. While inability to relate to abstract concepts may indeed be true for some individuals on the spectrum, it is by no means a taken-for-granted assumption that individuals on the spectrum cannot interpret the nuances of narrative.

Similarly, while I support Swinton's critique of commonly held assumptions in respect to autistic individuals' capacity for emotion, I find his own schemas of love to be perplexingly uncritically constructed. People love in a myriad of different ways. Some of those ways may indeed differ as a consequence of autism; however, Swinton's account assumes a universality in the way that people without autism are assumed to love that

I would contend does not exist. If it did, there would not be the multi-million pound industry of relationship self-help books, counselling and couples therapies; we would all understand one another's way of loving just fine on our own. Anyone who has ever been in a relationship, atypical or otherwise, would tell you that is sadly not the case. A useful illustration of this point is the success of the book *The Five Love Languages* by Gary Chapman (1992), which illustrates several common yet distinctive 'types' of love, and the importance of recognizing that one person's way of showing love and of needing to be loved may be markedly different from someone else's.

My son is remarkably emotionally perceptive. In the course of writing this book, he has stated many times and with genuine concern, 'You don't look happy.' He is not, self-admittedly, able to discern the context for others' emotions (in this context, 'not happy' perhaps better translates as 'stressed' or 'exhausted'), but he can see when others are distressed and this moves him. The mothers who shared their stories within this research would argue that their children are similarly loving, affectionate and responsive to moods. In this respect, I argue, Swinton not only generalizes neurotypical love as being overly romantic and sentimentalized, but overgeneralizes autistic love as being merely practical and unintuitive.

Swinton's model of theological response to disability generally, and autism specifically, seems to rely on the promise that 'God is love'. While this model promotes a model of unwavering acceptance and love towards all, I find it naively reductionist and frustratingly formulaic. Irrespective of whether the subject interest is Down's syndrome or autism, Swinton very often begins with insightful and nuanced criticisms of contemporary challenges to disability, yet ends with very uncritical and essentialist proclamations of Christian love. As I have demonstrated in Chapter 12, it is not enough to simply say that autistic individuals and their loved ones have a place in the Church simply because God loves them. As Jenny Lexhed so candidly proclaims, love is not enough.

While writing this book, I was asked what such a 'loving and hospitable' community might look like for parents of children with autism. This gave me considerable pause for thought. As I have shared above, those around us carried us onward on days when carrying on felt impossible. I am admittedly moved by (albeit arguably utopian) visions of a community that responds to the suffering of others by simply seeing and bearing with them. For parents, and particularly mothers, who often feel isolated and stigmatized by others' attitudes towards autism, and exhausted by its daily realities, the old adage that 'it takes a village to raise a child' holds particular significance. While that village may not, in reality, resemble Hauerwas's or Swinton's vision of 'Church', it offers an important reminder that we ought not to be alone in our particular struggles.

However, in the last chapter, both Abigail and Scarlet described challenges in obtaining acceptance and support for their children's conditions from within their own families, highlighting that even when relational ties are perceived to be fundamental and unconditional, they cannot always be counted upon to be so. Indeed, it has been some years since Micah has chosen to see his own father, who was unable to provide the consistency and stability that necessitates a place in Micah's life. Scarlet, too, struggled to forge the kind of co-parenting relationship necessary with her ex-husband to fully support their daughter together. Abigail and Naomi were both grateful to have supportive spouses to navigate their journey with, but they acknowledged that this often required a delicate balance of needs.

While it would be tempting to imagine a community in which our responsibilities and burdens were shared and supported equally, without judgement or expectation, in reality this is a thoroughly impractical, if not impossible, undertaking. It is often unfeasible for others to provide the kind of practical day-to-day support that mothers of children on the spectrum could genuinely benefit from. Those around me have often wished they could, but life is not so simple. Such compassion is a great thing. On days when we feel particularly burdened, the knowledge that another sees your struggle can be profoundly comforting. Such comfort, however, is arguably often fleeting when there is little respite from the struggle itself. In this sense,

I question how members of a community of solidarity might ameliorate the irresolvable, conflicting and deeply complex struggles of a lived experience that they themselves do not, and cannot, fully share.

Hauerwas situates himself as an outsider on the issue of disability, and so his interest in the subject, other than the context of his background in medical ethics, is unclear. Echoing criticisms Swinton has levelled at liberation theologies (Swinton, 2012a, p. 175), Nicholas Healey suggests that Hauerwas appears to be merely arbitrarily appropriating a social issue to further his particular agenda of demonstrating the uniqueness of the Church as a moral community (Healey, 2014, p. 5). Building on such critiques, Healey argues that such issues of academic privilege raise significant concerns as to the issue of authority in representing the voices of others within theology, proposing that Hauerwas's confessional rhetoric utilizes a sermon-like approach that disguises its deeply exclusionary aspects. I find that Swinton's conclusions similarly echo the rhetorical tone of Hauerwas's work that Healey finds deeply troubling, in that it asserts a liturgical authority that theological academic research typically does not, nor should have (Healey, 2014, p. 64).

Healey also raises concerns in respect to what he considers Hauerwas's universalization of 'the Church'. Denominations in different social locations and in different points in history vary so considerably that there is arguably no such thing as a universally accepted 'Church' or indeed the Christian formed in this church context. Healey contends that:

Formation is not simply a product of enacting a given set of practices. Persons are also formed by their reflections, discussions, and decisions about which practices to enact and how, as well as by their inevitable confusion over such matters. Our characters are constructed as the products of ongoing negotiations, whether explicitly or entirely un-reflected or somewhere in between. (Healey, 2014, p. 95)

In this sense, communitarian models that position the model of a 'hospitable community' as one that is distinctly and uniquely

Christian may present an uncritically constructed notion of both 'community' and the Christian person. It could be argued that there is nothing particularly or distinctly 'Christian' in the 'Christian character' Hauerwas describes; in fact, many non-Christians live similar lives with very similar values. For someone who themselves is outside this conception of 'Church', but who holds themselves accountable to many of the values Hauerwas purports to be exclusively Christian, I find this issue particularly problematic.

Developing a feminist liberation critique of Hauerwas's theology of communitarianism, Gloria Albrecht contends that communitarian theologies often neglect these inherent structural inequalities and hierarchies within the Christian community and assume a universality of experience and character that, as Althaus-Reid (2000, p. 18) and Goto (2018, p. 221) have identified, is often the experience of the white, Christian male. In the Introduction, I proposed that such dominant ideologies serve to hide the lived experiences of those who do not fit within such narrow models of knowledge.

Furthermore, while the communitarian model proposed recognizes the potential value of parental knowledge in respect to how we consider childhood disabilities, these models can often be seen to rely on the gender-neutral term 'parents' to describe what I will have intimated above – and will go on to argue – is a particularly gendered experience. I propose that caring for the needs of others, particularly in respect to children – and even more so when a child has additional support needs – is rather frequently 'a mother's burden'.

Albrecht suggests that Hauerwas's communitarian model of the family is premised upon traditional Christian archetypes that have particularly problematic implications for women (Albrecht, 1995, p. 56). Riet Bons-Storm observes that: 'Women in the Bible, like women who are treated according to the patriarchal sociocultural narrative, are to a great extent identified with their wombs, and yet do not have any authority over them' (Bons-Storm, 1996, p. 121). Elisabeth Schüssler Fiorenza furthers that the representation of women in the Bible as relationally defined by a male figure functions to preserve the structures and values of a paternalistic tradition, in which we are operating under a 'kyriarchal' system – that is, under the 'rule of the father/king/husband' (Schüssler Fiorenza, 1996, p. 3). This Christian 'marital blueprint', Albrecht argues, which has its roots in the Protestant Reformation, placed man as head of the household, and woman as his biological (and biblical) subordinate. The Lutheran social model of marriage exalted the ideals of piety, purity and docility for women, in which a woman's sense of purpose and fulfilment derived from performing her wifely, motherly, Christian duties (Daly, 1986, p. 85).

Such models of mothering assume a naturalness to mothering that is often far removed from the reality. The expectation of mothers to be all-giving, self-sacrificing, and delighted to be so, not only misrepresents the lived reality of mothering, but discounts mothers' experiences as a natural – and therefore unexceptional and taken-for-granted – way of being. Such misrepresentations can also be seen to significantly, and peculiarly, link mothering and autism in enduring and particularly damaging ways. In the following chapter, I will explore how mothers are uniquely implicated in historical, and indeed current, narratives of autism, examining how 'normative' expectations of mothering, coupled with symptomologies of autism that manifest in the 'everyday' routines of daily life, coalesce to create a distinct form of maternal struggle, and one that is thus distinctly theologically challenging.

Note

1 See https://www.gov.scot/publications/microsegmentation-autism-spectrum/pages/10/

PART 3

'Every day is a battle' – Mothers 'en la lucha'

.

We were squeezed into a very small office, the tension made more palpable by our physical closeness. I had requested this meeting, after weeks and months of phone calls, emails and daily logs in a 'behaviour book' passed from apologetic staff updating me on the ways in which my son was, ultimately, described as being 'unacceptable'.

My mother and I sat side by side, opposite the manager of the nursery that he attended. At first, his transgressions had been small – typical, I was assured, of a toddler boy. An occasional bite, a temper tantrum, a refusal to eat his lunch. However, these 'typicalities' slowly, and insidiously, became atypical. He would only eat or drink out of the one colour of plate and cup, and their attempts to break this habit resulted in abject fury, which would only be satiated upon return of his chosen items. He found the transitions between activities utterly impossible, refusing to abandon his task until he had completed it to his satisfaction. One particular member of staff bore the brunt of his aggressions, and this meeting followed an incident in which he had threatened her with scissors. He was almost four.

I expressed both my bewilderment, and concern, about his behaviour. I was, of course, deeply worried by the accusations levelled against him.

'I am quite worried, as I'm sure you are, about his behaviour. He is very close to beginning school, and I'd like to get to the bottom of this before he begins.'

What was perplexing to me was that, at the time at least, he did not display this level of aggression and defiance at home, nor indeed with other members of staff. His key worker had admitted that during external assessments, Micah (having an exceptional grasp of literacy and numeracy) was often the child they preferred to use to demonstrate their success. The boy I brought home, painted with on the floor, and read to sleep was quite different from the tumultuous, malicious boy depicted in his behaviour book. I shared this with the manager, not as a defence, but as an expression of bewilderment. I opened up his behaviour book, tracing my fingers down the entries.

'In his book, you can see there are patterns ... transition times, mealtimes, noisy activities ... At home, it is just us, and he has his own routine ... so possibly we are able to avoid some of the triggers he might have here, with other children? I really feel that it would be beneficial for Micah to be assessed, before he begins school? I'm concerned there might be something ... underlying in this behaviour?'

She bristled.

'Can I be frank, Ms Campbell?'

I could feel the storm rising within my mother at the emphasis she had placed on the 'Ms', but she held herself still. I nodded.

'Children are only able to release their emotions with people they feel safe with. Micah has had a full-time nursery placement since ... ten months old, correct? Quite honestly, he does not display this behaviour at home because he is never there. YOU are never there. You are at work, at university, but you're not with him. It is my opinion that what is underlying here, is emotional distress at his lack of bond with you.'

Those words rained down like sharp cuts, slicing, leaving me vulnerable, exposed. I could do nothing but sit there, chastised by my apparent and complete lack of mothering. Was she right? Was he suffering from neglect?

'Can I be frank?' My mother punctured the silence.

The manager, satisfied with her diagnosis, folded her arms across her chest. 'Of course.'

'If there were no working parents utilizing this nursery, you would have no children to look after. Correct? The only difference here is that my daughter is his only parent. Would we be having the same conversation if she were *sat here with a husband by her side, instead of as a single mother? I don't think that we would.'*

With that, she stood up. 'Thank you for your time. We will raise our concerns with the GP, so that someone qualified might make a less ... biased assessment.' We left the manager in stunned, outraged silence, the line in the sand drawn.

My mother held the door open for me, and I walked through it, numb from accusation. She gripped my hand, like I was a small child, and we were at once mother and child, and mother and mother.

13

Refrigerator Mothers:
Too Cold to Care?

My own experience of motherhood has been both everything I thought it would be, and nothing I thought it would be, simultaneously. I have found myself fitting seamlessly into some patterns of 'traditional' mothering, and joyfully so, while at the same time struggling against the pressures and constraints of others. Adrienne Rich writes: 'I told myself that I wanted to write a book on motherhood because it was a crucial, still relatively unexplored, area for feminist theory. But I did not choose this subject; it had long ago chosen me' (Rich, 1996, p. 15).

And so, too, has it chosen me. Decades have passed since Adrienne Rich published her book on the experience of motherhood, and yet her words ring as true today as they did some 40 years ago. Peculiarly, despite the fact that every person is, as Rich succinctly put it, 'of woman born', we seem reluctant to take motherhood as a subject of theoretical inquiry. Perhaps the universality of the condition of motherhood, the nature of motherhood as something apparently timeless, natural and necessary to society, has rendered it something taken for granted; we assume that motherhood simply is (Rich, 1996, p. 61). Motherhood is often, in contrast to fatherhood, termed 'an institution'. By definition, an institution is considered an establishment, or organization, that provides an important role or function to society. It carries with it the evocation of timelessness, of stability and durability. Rich observes:

When we think of an institution, we can usually see it as embodied in a building: the Vatican, the Pentagon, the Sorbonne, the Treasury, the Massachusetts Institute of Technology, the Kremlin, the Supreme Court ... When we think of the institution of motherhood, no symbolic architecture comes to mind, no visible embodiment of authority, power, or of potential or actual violence. Motherhood calls to mind home, and we like to believe that the home is a private place. (Rich, 1996, p. 274)

This symbolism of institution is problematic for women in several ways. The notion of institution evokes connotations of privacy, of important work done behind closed doors, crucial to society's function, and yet separate from it. This sense of 'hiddenness' has arguably obscured the experience of motherhood from social discourse, encouraging the perception that the act of mothering is restricted to the home and, as such, is a private and unspoken experience.

The privatization of motherhood was strongly influenced by the Industrial Revolution and changing attitudes towards child welfare, with women's wage-earning potential re-evaluated in favour of their child-rearing importance (Rich, 1996, p. 48). After World War Two, influential writers such as Will Durant constructed narratives that placed women and mothers as central to the continuation and rebuilding of 'civilization'. While exalting motherhood as crucial to the reconstruction of a civilized, peaceful society, Durant also strongly advocated adherence to 'traditional' relations between the sexes and women's domesticity within the home (Durant, 1946). This portrayal of a motherhood defined by domesticity and docility was enthusiastically adopted by the media at the time, disseminating a picture of motherhood in which mothers stayed at home, kept clean houses, well-used kitchens and happy children (Odland, 2010, p. 69).

At a time when society was fearful and exhausted from the trials of war, the effect of this vision was twofold: it provided a sense of comfort in the safety of the home, and also functioned to deter women from competing with men returning from war for the positions they occupied in their absence (Odland, 2010, p. 63). Familial separation and the desperate attempts to rebuild communities following the devastation of World Wars One and Two also led to a shift towards the home as the child's primary source of learning, with women being encouraged to actively engage with their child's mental and social development, to prioritize activities such as reading and play with their children so as to avoid the damaging effects of 'maternal deprivation' (Brown et al., 1994, p. 149). As a consequence, child development largely became the sole responsibility of the mother within the home. While historically women had felt the responsibility of being fruitful, of successfully bearing their husband's children, this shift in attitude towards the importance of 'nurture' now brought with it the pressure not only of mothering, but mothering well.

In my passage at the beginning of this chapter, I shared how this notion of 'mothering well' presents as insidiously challenging when in the context of children who present as 'different'. My own son's differences were attributed to my lack of mothering; his differences were, it was presumed, unequivocally my fault. This particular encounter shook my perception of myself as a mother to the core. Indeed, it has been almost a decade since, and despite the benefit of hindsight I can still feel those nagging thorns of blame under my skin. What I did not realize at the time, though, was that I was far from the first mother of an autistic child to be faced with such accusations.

In Chapter 1, I described the emergence of autism as credited to the observations of Dr Leo Kanner. More precisely, it was Kanner's reliance on comprehensive family histories in his diagnostic process that distinguished his work from that of his peers and solidified his place in history as 'discovering autism'. However, it would also be Kanner's casual observations of the parents themselves that would form the basis of one of the most enduring and damaging claims in the history of autism. The complex interrelation of social impairments presented by children with autism was undoubtedly extremely difficult to navigate for the parents seeking Kanner's assistance. Arguably, it was this desperation that led them to Kanner in the first place. What they had likely not anticipated, however, was the extent to which they themselves would feature in their children's diagnosis:

> I have dwelt at some length on the personalities, attitudes, and behaviour of the parents because they seem to throw considerable light on the dynamics of the children's psychopathologic condition ... patients were exposed from the beginning to parental coldness, obsessiveness, and a mechanical type of attention to material needs only ... They were kept neatly in refrigerators which did not defrost. (Kanner, 1943, p. 425)

Kanner's nuanced observations of his patients' complex behaviours were punctuated by very personal (and arguably clinically baseless) observations of the psychology of their parents – or, more precisely, their mothers. The association between high intellect in mothers and their autistic children were ones that were to be echoed by Hans Asperger as an unusual commonality; however, Kanner's perception of the link between parental intelligence and autistic traits was much less favourable. While such descriptions would most likely fail to pass as legitimately credible clinical observation today, Kanner's depiction of these mothers was unquestionably accepted at the time.

While this hampered any deeper investigation into the causality of autism, it also served to keep autism within the field of psychiatry and, consequently, within the remit of Kanner himself. Thus autism was regarded as a psychological condition, and therefore one that could be treated. Furthermore, in associating autism with mothering, Kanner tapped into a popular social anxiety at the time – that of women entering the workforce. Bruno Bettelheim, psychologist and contemporary of Kanner, popularized this perception of the 'refrigerator mother' with publications such as *Why Mothers Feel Guilty* and *The Empty Fortress*. Capitalizing on the fear that further education and the economic independence of women during the war would destroy the traditional family, Bettelheim propelled Kanner's theory into the mainstream media and created a damning culture of blame that cited women as the cause of their own family's demise. Psychologist and leading researcher in autism Uta Frith observes that:

> This caricature of bad mothering overlaps with the caricature of the career woman, in particular the 'intellectual' type. An abnormally detached child – a child who is unable to relate lovingly – is a fitting punishment for the woman who neglected to be a full-time devoted wife and mother! (Frith, 2003, p. 30)

Kanner's damning indictment of the 'refrigerator mother' fuelled this assumed divide between 'good' and 'bad' mothers, contributing to a damaging culture of maternal guilt. This created an impossible situation for mothers: if they sought help for their children, they were subjected to blame and stigma; if they did not, they were forced to ignore their concerns and forgo any possible assistance they might have accessed for their child. McGuire observes that in situating 'blame' with mothers, such discourses unavoidably place mothers in the untenable position of having to pathologize their child, to highlight and emphasize the difference in them, in order to rid themselves of blame. Bernard Rimland, author of *Early Infantile Autism* and parent to an autistic boy himself, wrote of Kanner's assertion:

> To add a heavy burden of shame and guilt to the distress of people whose hopes, social life, finances, well-being and feelings of worth have been all but destroyed seems heartless and inconsiderate in the extreme. (Rimland, 1965, p. 65)

In the case of autism, mothers are thus uniquely affected by, and implicated in, the condition in a number of complex and interrelating ways. Despite the years that have elapsed, the effects of Kanner's damning indictment of the 'refrigerator mother' continue to taint our perception of autism. McGuire observes that this popular depiction of mothers was also that of the white, middle-class, bourgeois mother. Such mothers, it was assumed, were naturally imbued with the capacity to mother 'correctly'. In contrast, mothers who were poor, racialized, or disabled were presumed to be inherently deficient in their capacity to mother, in need of the child-rearing guidance of predominantly middle-class, white men (McGuire, 2016, p. 40). Perhaps incongruously, Kanner's depiction of the educated, white, middle-class mother cited exactly these desirable traits as contributing to their child's pathology, while the former (the poor, racialized and disabled) were excluded from the blame of autism (and, consequently, of a diagnosis at all) by the supposition that they were simply not intelligent enough. Research has shown that this racial, and indeed economic, divide still exists, with children from marginalized backgrounds statistically less likely to obtain a diagnosis.

While awareness and understanding of autism has increased in recent decades, discrediting notions that autism is a psychological disturbance caused by mothers, the painful legacy of these models can arguably continue to be seen in the way mothers experience the diagnostic process, access support, and are treated socially. Nicholas and colleagues observe that throughout the literature the stereotype of what makes a 'good mother', and the strict conditions under which one may adhere to this category, remain a significant cause of stress among mothers of children on the autism spectrum (Nicholas et al., 2016, p. 927). The expectation of being 'the good mother' may result in a comparative self-assessment of motherhood, with mothers measuring their perceived success or failure at caring for their children's needs comparative to those of 'typically' developing children (Gill and Liamputtong, 2011). Abigail considered her ability to cope with her children not in terms of comparison with other mothers, but in her own expectations of herself being challenged by the situations she faced with her daughter:

> You doubt yourself. You do, you doubt yourself. To some extent I felt a failure. I'm letting her down. And to some extent I couldn't cope because her behaviour as a teenager really did get excessive. We had lots of self-harming. We had lots of suicidal ideation. We had smoking, we had drinking.

At one point she tried to exit a moving vehicle when the car was going at 60 mph ... And in the midst of it, you've got a psychiatrist saying she's just doing it to wind her mother up. So as a mother you think what am I doing that's causing her to want to wind me up this much? So it's really, really hard.

While Kanner's psychology of maternal blame has been strongly discredited since the 1940s, more recent genetic research has suggested that the presence of a 'broad autistic phenotype' may be visible in the form of milder social inconsistencies in mothers of children on the autism spectrum (Duerte et al., 2005, p. 417). Clara Claiborne Park and Jenny Lexhed both noted that they themselves 'fit the criteria' of Kanner and Asperger's high-achieving, academic parents. In writing this, I would be naïve not to recognize elements of myself within this profile. The mothers I spoke with were similarly aware of the link assumed between autism and maternal biology; however, they all regarded this with considerable pragmatism. Naomi observed that she actually took comfort in the research; in considering the association as something medical rather than behavioural, the potential link almost took away the question of 'blame' for her son's behaviour:

> Eventually, the more I researched the more I realized it wasn't my fault, it was neurological, it wasn't within my control. Even if someone had said, if you do this, this and this in pregnancy, you'll have a child with autism I still wouldn't change it because he is who he is and what will be will be. It's hard to describe ... I'm not guilt-ridden now but back then I was.

Vera noted that her sister also had children on the spectrum and discussed the similarities she observed between her daughter and herself at her age, considering the likenesses advantageous to her understanding of her daughter: 'It's like having a built-in guide book.' Abigail commented that while biological causes were not something that she considered before having children, nor did she lament the fact that an established link could be seen in their family, these may be factors that affect her daughter's view on motherhood in the future:

When you have children you don't plan ... I'm going to have kids that are on the spectrum. You don't plan that. Maybe now it's different for my daughter, because she knows that she has a diagnosis, her brother has a diagnosis. My children are to two different biological dads, and she knows that we reckon my dad is on the spectrum, so she sees that it's going down my bloodline. So she has to think to herself, 'when I have kids, I may be facing kids that are on the spectrum'. So it may be different for her.

Our accounts add weight to the (what is arguably now prevailing) theory that autism can be shown to have a genetic component. We were all able to identify things in ourselves or quirks and 'eccentricities' within the family line that made themselves visible in our children. Rather than demonstrating the hereditary aspect of autism as a symptom of nurture, Hoffman and colleagues (2009) counter the assumption that potential genetic components correlate with the stereotype of Kanner's 'autistic parenting'. In a study of attachment in mothers of children with autism, he found that maternal closeness and attachment was not shown to be any different to that of mothers of typically developing children, dispelling the notion of 'the refrigerator mother'. Certainly, a lack of love is far from present in the mothers of ASD children I have encountered. Rather, I would argue that we perhaps sometimes love too fiercely, because we have to love our children even harder in the light of what can often be the unloving gazes of others.

A mother's love?

Dominant discourses that romanticize the experience of motherhood as something biological, natural and altruistic have caused the conflicts of mothering to be silenced, hidden and neglected from any real critical enquiry. Perhaps more significantly, mothers struggle against an insidiously dominant discourse which suggests that women who experience struggle in their motherhood are somehow 'anti-woman', unnatural and uncredible. Bons-Storm argues that we are unreliable witnesses to our own testimony (Bons-Storm, 1996, p. 18). In earlier pages I have also articulated an experience of mothers that is similarly and dangerously silenced.

We are all too often mothers conflicted by the traditional narratives of what motherhood is assumed to be, in contrast to the reality of motherhood as we truly live it. I have caught glimpses of myself and others on the pages of Adrienne Rich (1976), Riet Bons-Storm (1996) and Bonnie Miller-McLemore (1994) as they bravely revealed the unthinkable, much less nameable – that mothers are not always brimming with love and patience and utterly fulfilled by their children; but, rather, mothers are often conflicted, exhausted and drained by the ceaseless demands and expectations of motherhood. I have admitted my own complicity in this silence by being reluctant to share how overwhelmed and exhausted I have often felt in my role as a mother. Adrienne Rich, writing candidly on the physical and emotional toll of motherhood, asks us:

> What woman, in the solitary confinement of a life at home enclosed with young children, or in the struggle to mother them while providing for them single-handedly, or in the conflict of weighing her own personhood against the dogma that says she is a mother, first, last, and always – what woman has not dreamed of going over the edge, of simply letting go, relinquishing what is termed her sanity so that she can be taken care of for once, or can simply find a way to take care of herself? (Rich, 1996, p. 279)

While Wolfteich contends that Rich 'speaks over women who may interpret mothering in terms of sacrality, vocation, or empowerment', she notes that 'mothering can be a site of oppression and/or freedom, suffering and/or fulfilment', and that these conflicts are currently ignored theologically (Wolfteich, 2017, pp. 141, 145). Where such conflicts *are* considered, Bonnie Miller-McLemore suggests that they often draw from unhelpful theologies of 'agape' or 'altruistic love', which harmfully reinforce unrealistic representations and expectations of maternal experience (Miller-McLemore, 1994, p. 102). Such theologies of motherhood portray women as adopting their child-rearing responsibilities with a self-sacrificing commitment and seemingly limitless love for their children; however, in reality, this is by no means a natural state and by no means a constant state of being. Miller-McLemore observes:

> Not only is loving sacrifice impossible as a goal, it denies women the complex realities of maternal labour – that a good mother can sometimes hate her children, that a mother may love her children, but hate mothering, that vesting one person with full responsibility for mothering may not be wise, or even possible. (Miller-McLemore, 1994, p. 164)

I have shared my deep unease at academic efforts to 'theologize' love, particularly when such attempts may provoke universalized and unhelpful stereotypes of loving. Mothers, like anyone else, lose patience. We become tired, and at times we may even feel overwhelmed and resentful of the demands of our children. Presenting mothers as endless and virtuously giving, Bons-Storm asserts, creates a dangerous expectation on mothers' abilities to continue to give beyond their means:

> Most women are rightly convinced that many persons around them are in need of kindness and loving care. So they give it. Only there is no limit to the giving. To stop or to limit the caring and giving would mean to stop playing a role that is seen as their destiny as women. (Bons-Storm, 1996, p. 61)

I have already highlighted that in respect to autism such damaging and unhelpful stereotypes of mothers as virtuously giving have simultaneously functioned to inhibit research into autism itself by laying blame with unaffectionate mothers, and also significantly impacted mothers' ability to voice the struggles and challenges of their experiences in fear of being considered 'not loving enough'. Miller-McLemore proposes that such theologies also support the perception that self-sacrificing love is what is necessarily *distinct* about mothers and their abilities (Miller-McLemore, 1994, p. 104). In my reflection that precedes this chapter, I have described an encounter with a support agency that could arguably be seen to be shaped by this very misconception. The belief that mothers can, not least should, be able to manage whatever challenges their children present stoically and without complaint can in very real terms be seen to continue to shape provision of support at an institutional level for mothers of children with autism.

For such mothers, caring demands are exhausting, unrelenting and leave little time for considerations of mothers' own well-being. Clare Wolfteich, drawing on Patricia Hill Collins's term 'motherwork', rejects the popular assumption that maternal conflicts lie in the 'balance' between work and motherhood. Rather, she asserts, only when we acknowledge 'mothering as work and to mothering in relationship to other spheres of women's labour' will we begin to see that women's roles are interconnected and often indivisible (Wolfteich, 2017, p. 6). However, as Miller-McLemore notes:

> ... there is nothing automatic or natural about any of this. Caring for children requires deep conserves of energy, extended periods of patience, and a heightened intellectual activity that has seldom been recognised as such. Moreover, the spiritual potential of living with children only comes when the spirituality of everyday life is recognised, affirmed, and attended to as being equally worthy with fasting and praying. Then, the sometimes tedious, sometimes wondrous intricacices of 'caring labour' for another – dressing, nursing, feeding, cleaning, wiping, brushing, guarding, protecting, reprimanding, teaching, watching, following, listening, mediating, responding and anointing the head of a child – teaches something nameless that is nonetheless essential to life and to living. (Miller-McLemore, 1994, p. 158)

This extract highlights that while the 'everyday' acts of caring labour are often assumed to be natural, automatic and taken-for-granted daily actions for mothers, they are in fact conscious, deliberate and considered acts that illustrate the distinct qualities of mothers. In this respect, I believe that the 'everydayness' of mothering is not merely instinctive, but is rather intentional, and requires a deep attention to the often conflicting demands of everyday life. In the next chapter, I will examine how such conflicting demands present themselves in the 'everydayness' of living with autism, identifying a distinct form of maternal struggle that is manifest in the seemingly mundane, banal and everyday acts of daily living. Such struggles are often profound, even traumatic, yet they also hold deep theological potential.

He would not put his shoes on. He couldn't tell me why, other than that they were 'terrible'. As were the boots, the sandshoes and, in desperation, the trainers I attempted to wrestle him into. He would not wear shoes EVER, he told me. His anger was sudden and disproportionate. We sat on the stairs, at an impasse; him, furious, me utterly bewildered. Eventually, I steeled myself. 'I am your mother, and you MUST go to school.'

He was only five. The shoe issue had arisen suddenly and unexpectedly. In those first days, I had spoken to him softly, reassuringly, attempting to distract him with tales of all the fun he would have at school once he arrived. When it became clear that my reassurances were mistrusted, I tried games. Putting his shoes first on his teddies, then on our dog (this elicited a brief and bewildered repose from his rage), then, lastly, and unsuccessfully, on him. We had bought new shoes, with dinosaurs (his obsession) and flashing lights. While he appreciated these in the store, in abstract, he most certainly did not appreciate them in the context of his own feet. Day after day, he roared in fury. He threw things. He banged his head repeatedly on the floor. He sobbed, disconsolate. I tried everything.

Eventually, arduously, I managed to wrangle him into a pair of shoes, sweating, exhausted by the effort. While he clung to the banister, howling in rage, I repeated this mantra to myself 'You MUST go to school.' That's what good mothers did. They got their children dressed and they took them to school. I gripped his tiny hand and forced us through the door. We were fortunate enough to live only a few minutes' walk from school. It's only along the street. We were out of the house, that was always the hardest part. We would make it.

Immediately, he flung himself to the ground, anchoring his tiny body to the spot, and screamed. In panic, pain-

fully aware of the stream of other parents and children we would soon join, I scooped him up, his body contorting and twisting in anger. I staggered resolutely onwards, trying desperately to ignore the onslaught of blows as he writhed furiously in my arms. The bell had long since rung and, mercifully, only a handful of parents remained on the street, their chatting quietening to shocked silence at our approach. We pushed forward. He kicked, he punched. He twisted fistfuls of hair. He bit. He spat. And still, we were not yet there. Then one furious punch brought a turret of blood from my nose, the next tearing the flesh of my lip in two. I stopped, frozen. He froze, too, the sight of my blood jolting him out of his rage and dissolving him into complete devastation.

I sat down on the ground, enveloping his now sobbing limbs in mine. I held him, and I rocked him, tears streaming silently down my face. 'It's OK', I shushed. 'I'm OK, you're OK. We're OK.' Over and over. I rocked him. I don't know how long we sat there like that, he and I. I lost all awareness of the silent stares of the other parents; at some point they had abandoned our spectacle and returned to their day. By the time his sobs had quietened, and his body stilled, the street was empty. I lifted him to his feet, clutching his hand and walked finally, brokenly, to the school office.

The door opened and the secretary looked up from her desk. Her mouth fell open. She disappeared through a door. I looked up, staring at our reflection in the glass doors. My hair was a tangled nest, my face filthy and streaked with blood and tears. My son was ashen, hollow-eyed, exhausted. We stood there, broken, shattered by trauma. A minute later, she reappeared, teacher in tow. The teacher, though visibly alarmed, looked at us with a mixture of sympathy and concern. We stared back, unable to speak.

'Oh dear,' she said. 'I think Mum needs a cup of tea.' She turned to the secretary, 'Can you take Micah to wash his face please?'

His little hand tightened on mine, and my mouth opened to protest.

'He is OK. Right now, you're the one who needs to be looked after. Come with me.'

I nodded, still unable to speak. My stubborn attempts to conceal my private struggle had been laid bare. There was no hiding any more.

14

A Mother's Work is Never Done: Struggle in the Everyday

What has emerged in the book this far is a distinct and complex lived experience that presents an equally complex and distinct theological challenge. In sharing our stories, it is clear that mothers face unusual and particular struggles in their experience of mothering children on the autism spectrum, shaped by complex and often conflicting social and political debates on disability. While the theologies of disability explored in previous chapters could be seen to address some of these issues; I found that such theologies did not relate to everyday lived experience, nor to the interconnected nature of the competing social discourses that affected our everyday lives.

Mothers, I have argued, are most typically the primary caregivers of children generally, and atypical children particularly. Therefore, I consider the absence of attention to maternal experience within disability theology to be peculiar at best and, at worst, a missed theological opportunity. I believe that the distinct experience of mothers of children on the spectrum is one that is even more significantly ignored in the research, yet it has the potential to provoke a particularly new and insightful form of theological thinking. The question then arises, what is distinct about the particular experience of maternal struggle that I have revealed, and how do we respond to it theologically? This has proven to be more challenging than the question I initially expected to answer.

While considering this issue my son asked me, with learned thoughtfulness, 'What bit are you working on now, Mama?' 'Struggle,' I sighed, contemplatively. 'How are you getting on?'

he asked. I laughed. 'I'm struggling.' He paused for a moment. This pause invariably means one of two things from an eleven-year-old boy – he is either considering whether or not this is interesting enough for him to pursue the conversation, or he is choosing an appropriate social response to bring me some measure of comfort in my admission. Eventually he also sighed and said, 'Well, you see the irony here.' Who says autists do not understand abstract concepts?

In the course of our lives, I would anticipate that we have all, at one point or another, considered ourselves '*Pues, ahi, en la lucha*', or 'in the struggle', when asked how we are doing (Isasi-Díaz, 2004, p. 229). The mothers in this book have all, at one point or another, been told 'I don't know how you do it' in response to their answer on their well-being. This is problematic in a number of ways. It is a closed question – or, rather, it is a statement rather than a question. It leaves little scope when trying to respond. It in effect asserts that they know nothing of your struggle, but also shuts down the invitation to share it. It is, I assume, intended to convey a recognition of our struggle but also our resilience. However, this presents a simplistic kind of sympathy, which is often experienced more as pity than empathy. And so, in response to those who exclaim 'I don't know how you do it', this book has tried to find a way of explaining.

As mothers of children on the autism spectrum, in the course of sharing our lived experiences with one another, we all laughed and cried together when considering this statement; we all agreed that we were, quite simply, struggling. It also became alarmingly clear that while at a surface level literature alluded to autism as presenting 'unique challenges' to daily living, these challenges were often listed arbitrarily, with very little critical examination of how such challenges are really lived and experienced for mothers. In what follows, I will explore this lived experience within the context of theologies that focus on the complexity of struggles that are rooted in the seemingly mundane practice of everyday living, before considering the contribution of feminist theologies that acknowledge the significance of motherhood as a profound source of knowledge.

In shifting away from theologies of disability, towards theologies that focus on women's lived experience, I will examine
whether such theologies may be better placed to offer a more
nuanced response to the particularity of the lived experiences
that have emerged within this book as a distinct form of
maternal struggle.

The everyday: a site of struggle and resistance

Being 'passionately engaged in life's struggle' is very often
most strongly demonstrated in the 'everydayness' of life as we
live it. The experiences of myself and the other women who
have shared their stories have highlighted that our struggles
are most often fought day to day. While we are acutely aware
of the 'bigger picture' in respect to school placements, continuing access to resources, and the impending reality of 'ageing
out' of support provision,[1] these larger issues are often forced
to be peripheral to the intricacy and immediacy of the daily
planning required to be responsive to our children's needs. For
mothers of children on the spectrum, even seemingly inconsequential everyday acts such as dressing, or remembering to buy
the right brand of something, can have profound significance
and meaning for our children and, by extension, for ourselves.
The symptoms of autism play out in the myriad of taken-
for-granted spheres of 'normal' daily living; from eating and
sleeping to speaking and hearing. Autism is invisible, yet tan-
gibly pervasive in the ways in which it manifests in everyday
life – and distinctly problematic when considered in respect of
theologies of inclusion and adaptation.

Critiquing the 'personal tragedy model' of disability, Sarah
Green found that parents of children with autism were much
more significantly impacted by the objective realities of exhaustion and financial struggles associated with daily caregiving
(Green, 2007, p. 161). The mothers I spoke with were at pains
to reinforce the fact that their children were not sources of
sadness for them – nor even necessarily their condition – but,
rather, it was facing the complex, unexpected and ever-changing

challenges and social barriers that autism brought to their lives that was the problem. However, while I find the premise of Green's article "'We're tired, not sad'" particularly useful in challenging the personal tragedy stereotype of 'struggle', I am wary that it may neglect the multiplicity of the challenges associated with autism mothering. In respect to autism – and, I would counter, disabilities more generally – our subjective and objective realities are very often mutually reinforcing entities. This frames the challenge of mothering of children on the spectrum as a 'double burden' that is particularly difficult for women.

Many of the issues that autistic individuals find challenging are often counterintuitive to the realities of social life, such as the need for routine and stability – along with other somewhat unpredictable challenges arising from disrupted sleep patterns, restricted diet, sensory sensitivity to noise, busyness, strong smells. These problems are often framed under the innocuous heading 'problems with personal independence'. This implies that such problems are indeed personal to the child, when in reality they are profoundly impactful for those who care for them. In the Prologue to this book, I described a night of sleeplessness, broken and exhausted by being unable to soothe my baby. While many mothers generally will be all too grimly familiar with such nights, it has been shown that with children on the spectrum the inability to form a sleep pattern extends beyond infancy. Now that my son is older, I am often asked by exhausted new mothers when my child started to sleep, desperate for some light at the end of the tunnel for their sleep-refusing babies. When I tell them he was four, it is without exaggeration.

While now, mercifully, Micah will sleep soundly through the night, I have learned that he is somewhat the exception and not the rule. John Gillibrand shares a particularly heart-wrenching description of his and his wife's decision to seek residential support for their son, following days of constant nightly vigilance over him (Gillibrand, 2009, p. 43). Scarlet reflected similarly, sharing that her daughter's sleeplessness was so severe that she was eventually prescribed melatonin. However, she recalls with frustration that the knowledge that this was something she could ask for was not made available, and so she endured years of wakened nights watching over her daughter. My mother used to say (often when she was relieving me for an evening) that you can cope with anything on a good night's sleep. While a body will inevitably adapt to receiving minimum rest, the effects of constant exhaustion inhibit an ability to cope. Naomi cited exhaustion as being one of the biggest challenges to her daily life:

> The lack of sleep. He doesn't sleep. That has a major impact, because it impacts school, it impacts my health because I don't sleep because he's not sleeping. He's okay, because he seems to get enough that he needs. But I'm constantly exhausted. And I have two other children. And a house to run and meals to cook and the meetings and dog walking and more meetings ... everything you can imagine. It affects so many different parts.

In *Mujerista Theology,* Ada María Isasi-Díaz reflects on a seemingly inconsequential moment at a bus stop with a young mother. She observed that the woman's son was smartly dressed and appeared clean, healthy and well cared for. In contrast, the mother was visibly exhausted, dishevelled, holding a takeaway coffee and a doughnut that was probably her breakfast. While many would have merely glanced at the duo and moved on, Isasi-Díaz was struck by the many conflicting decisions that woman likely had to make that morning (Isasi-Díaz, 2011, p. 52). Was she drinking takeaway coffee because her income, rather than her time, did not allow for the luxury of buying enough groceries for her to eat breakfast at home? Had they only enough water to wash her son and his clothes? Is she exhausted from the competing demands of working to support him, and being present enough to meet his needs? Isasi-Díaz affirms that while we can often be seen to struggle as a result of major life circumstances and the effect of these, the reality of such struggles cannot be detached from the seemingly unremarkable practices of everyday life. The 'big stuff', she contends, affects the 'little stuff', but it is the 'little stuff' that can often feel the biggest struggle.

Isasi-Díaz's observation echoes the difficult and unseen challenges shared by Naomi and I. Our mornings were dictated by a myriad of seemingly tiny decisions and battles that had to be waged simply to get our children to school. The daily issues in our lives were significant sources of struggle that were peculiar to our particular context. In this sense, we were keenly aware of the reality that Isasi-Díaz goes on to admit: that she, much like the other mothers at the school gate, occupied a position of privilege in which mornings were easy, and tough decisions simply didn't have to be made (Isasi-Díaz, 2011, p. 55). Naomi gave the example of the seemingly unimportant number of yoghurts in the fridge:

> It's the same with taking his meds in the morning – he takes his meds with the same yoghurt every morning. But if someone else eats that yoghurt the whole day erupts. But it's their home too, so I can't tell the girls 'don't eat his yoghurts'.

While for many mothers the matter of not having enough yoghurts could be considered a minor inconvenience, for mothers of children with autism a simple yoghurt can be fraught with hidden meanings and far-reaching implications that would seem impossible for anyone else to consider significant. Such narratives are often framed within the literature as 'caregiving demands' or 'disruptions to daily living'. Certainly, they are both. However, what I consider significant about Naomi's particular reflection is that it highlights that one of the significant challenges of autism is that the 'simple' is very rarely 'simple'; the mundane is often interwoven with the complex, and tiny changes can result profoundly on how the day will transpire. Put simply, what is easy for others can be a monumental struggle for those of us with children on the spectrum.

For my son, dressing represented his most monumental struggle. This I came to regard with a degree of irony – of all the triggers we could potentially avoid, putting clothes on was not one of them. He would only wear certain clothes; finding the right ones was an arduous process of trial and error, and once found they had to be bought in bulk, in various sizes, because his need for sameness was all-consuming to him. Sensory sensitivity scored particularly highly in his diagnosis, and this manifested in his inability to tolerate certain textures on his skin. Temple Grandin, in her autobiography *Emergence: Labeled Autistic*, describes her own struggles with tactile sensitivity, which was at times overwhelmingly unbearable for her to manage. She recalls one particular incident in which she causes her mother to crash their car over her inability to tolerate the sensation of a sunhat on her head:

> My ears felt as if they were being squashed together into one giant ear. The band of the hat pressed tightly into my head. I jerked the hat off and screamed. Screaming was my only way of telling Mother that I didn't want to wear the hat. It hurt. (Grandin, 1996, p. 12)

This example is particularly useful as it highlights that something seemingly innocuous and harmless to Temple's mother, a simple sunhat, is utterly devastating to Temple. When a neurotypical individual chooses clothing, we will typically select our garments based on style, colour or aesthetic. While we may have a preference of fabric, our decision to wear or not wear a particular item is rarely determined by whether or not our skin can tolerate the sensation of it. For someone with autism, the sensation of the wrong garment can be almost incapacitating.

The cause of such sensory sensitivity among autistic individuals is unknown. While early theories suggested a 'compensatory model', proposing that individuals with autism favoured certain stimuli such as taste, touch and smell to the detriment of others, this was dispelled as increasing evidence observed sensory difficulties among all five senses, with no discernible trend or pattern (Frith, 2003, p. 169). Rather, Frith suggests that instead there is a difference in the way that those with autism process certain stimuli, rather than necessarily the stimuli themselves. She suggests a hypothesis of 'stimulus over selectivity', which argues that 'autistic children cannot attend well to simultaneously presented information and therefore select one narrow aspect of this information' (Frith, 2003, p. 170). It has also been suggested that external stimuli are often unpredictable and difficult to control, and therefore can be a source of anxiety for individuals with autism. Certainly, in a world in which we are confronted with unexpected and often competing stimuli, the experience of the autistic individual is one of constant external assault.

Conversely, similar to the sensory self-stimulation I touched upon in Chapter 3, the *right* sensory inputs are thought to have a compensatory effect in supressing the nervous system's reaction to over-stimulation. While my son could not tolerate anything loose or baggy on him, he liked to wear his clothing too small, which provided him with the tightness he so desired. To this end, his clothing had to be tight to the point of marking his tiny body, leaving grooves, indents and often bruises. This was soothing to him, reassuring. However, it often drew curious and intrusive stares: was he neglected? Could we not afford new clothes?

Consumed with an irrational fear of laces coming undone or Velcro snapping and causing him to trip (this has in fact never happened, but the possibility of it was enough), coupled with the need to have his clothing grip his body, Micah rejected every pair of shoes we attempted to put on him until eventually deciding on a pair of leather buckled sandals. Now that he is older, he reminisces with good humour about what has gone down in family folklore as 'The Year of the Sandal'. These beloved sandals, bought at the beginning of spring, we considered a success. However, by the December, and on our eighth pair of what had to be the same brand and model of sandal (which had long been discontinued and that we now had to source by ever more creative means), this seemingly small victory had become the focus around which Micah oriented the success or failure of his day, and consequently ours.

I vividly remember during the challenging period mentioned in my previous reflection watching other mothers at the school gates, wondering what they would consider a 'bad morning' … what would it be like, I wondered, for my child to simply get dressed in the morning? Smile and wave at me at the school gates? Sometimes, I would be able to laugh at the absurdity of how traumatic the loss of a particular sock could be for us; at other times, I would weep with something akin to bitter injustice that such mundane, seemingly simple, daily occurrences were never simple. In admitting this to Naomi, she revealed that she had witnessed my daily battle of the school run and had shared much of it herself with her own son. Later in our conversation she confessed that she too felt burdened by daily life:

> Every day is a struggle. Mainly on me, but Ryan has the financial burden ... nobody realizes the financial burden. I genuinely think if he didn't work away and earn a good wage I don't know where we'd be ... it's so hard because it feels like a constant battle, you're up and down to the school, you're taking it home, and then my husband and I were just bickering as well ... which didn't help the situation at all. Other people would always say how smiley I was, but people had no idea.

Naomi's account highlights that the ability to navigate these daily battles often restricted us to the 'domestic sphere'; the time demands of appointments, alternative educational paths, and crises often superseded our ability to maintain our careers. Scarlet and Naomi both spoke of being unable to continue working as a result of the frequency and inflexibility of appointments, and the high number of absences from school. Naomi admitted, 'I thought I'd be a qualified nurse by now, but it hasn't worked out that way. But he comes first and that's the way it is.'

As I shared in Chapter 7, my son was unable to cope with organized childcare – or, rather, they were unable to cope with him. I have been fortunate enough to largely be able to structure my work and research around his schooling; however, it has been a delicate, intensely stressful and exhausting balancing act. Every successful balance has come as a consequence of sacrifice; my progression in both my academic and working career has, in some respects, undoubtedly been impeded by my inability to commit to full-time hours, attend conferences, or be flexible in my schedule. Moreover, in addition to practical constraints, there are cognitive limits to what we are able to manage. In a study examining the lived experience of mothers of children on the spectrum, Nicholas and colleagues found that among their respondents mothers described that, along with additional caring needs, they also had *anticipatory* caring requirements that occupied their thinking. Describing the necessity of pre-empting potential triggers or difficulties with proactive and often ever-changing solutions, they note that autism was observed to be 'pervasive' in the thoughts, structures and routines of mothers:

> ... unlike a job with delineated working hours and designated tasks, the roles of these mothers were described as broad-based and 'all encompassing', and were thought to vastly exceed the demands associated with mothering a typically developing child. Participants described unending demands which required anticipatory planning for events in and out of the home, continual monitoring and adjustment, ongoing ingenuity and work in addressing the child's immediate and anticipated needs, and responding to challenges in proactive ways. (Nicholas et al., 2016, p. 926)

The pervasiveness of 'anticipatory planning' in my thoughts and routines is one that I have personally struggled with. I am not a natural planner. Organization is something I enthusiastically attempt, only to abandon it as everyday life gets in the way. In mothering a child with autism, you cannot just be two steps ahead, but five. Once you learn to speak the complex language of all the anxieties your child may struggle with daily, which is in and of itself a long and often cyclical process, you then begin to pre-empt the myriad of potential triggers and situations that may derail their equilibrium. His favourite things must always, always be carried in twos – for if one were to break, the consequences would be unthinkable.

As a lone parent with a small baby, I had relied upon routines because it simply made things easier; as an older child, these routines became less convenient and more crucial to his well-being. For my part, this was a considerable source of emotional disruption. While some strategies could be relied upon to be consistent, I was regularly confounded by situations arising that circumvented my meticulous planning. I would frequently receive calls from school about seemingly trivial occurrences: his juice has spilled on his trousers, the corner of his drawing has ripped, his lunch 'smells funny'. While perhaps most children would be able to brush off these frustrations, Micah would often be unable to continue with his day. When this occurred, it was often dispiriting and overwhelming, leaving me feeling like a failure for being unable to anticipate every eventuality. The ceaselessness of anticipating the possible multiple meanings everyday objects or activities may have for Micah was profoundly exhausting.

However, the consequences of failing to pre-empt such triggers were severe. The reflection I described earlier was not an isolated incident but was to become a routine part of our morning for many, many months. As recently as a few weeks ago, a neighbour of mine, remarking on how much my son had grown, commented: 'I remember when you used to have to carry him to school, you'll not be doing that now ... What a hard time he used to give you.' It was well-intended, but this encounter reminded me that while, mercifully, it has been many years since I have had to carry him to school, our school run was so traumatic that it remains not just in our memories, but in others' memories. His behaviour was unpredictable, unexpected and often uncharacteristically violent. Indeed, it was partly as a consequence of these seemingly unmitigated, and often very public, acts of violence that a referral for diagnosis was prompted.

In 'Autistic psychopathy in childhood', Hans Asperger offers a detailed description of what he termed 'autistic acts of malice' which his patients displayed towards their caregivers, peers, environment and self. 'These acts,' he muses, 'typically appear to be calculated. With uncanny certainty, the children manage to do whatever is the most unpleasant or hurtful in a particular situation' (1944, translated in Frith, 1991, p. 77).

This description is particularly jarring. It assumes not only an inherent cruelty in the autistic individuals observed but also an awareness of the cruelty of their acts. On their worst days, parents and caregivers of children with autism may sometimes feel the resonance of Asperger's words and attribute intent to the autistic aggression they are experiencing. This can consequently have a profound and severely damaging impact on relationships and family life – with parents facing the additional stress of being at risk of being injured by their child, and also in preventing their child from harming themselves. Abigail spoke of a particularly distressing encounter with her own daughter:

> There was one night I was bringing her home, I can't remember after what or what happened, but whatever happened she wasn't happy about what was said in the car and when we got home, she stormed up the stairs and said, 'I won't be here in the morning,' and shut the door. We had to bust the door in ... Children on the spectrum struggle to vocalize their emotions at the best of times, so asking her if she's going to be there in the morning ... she's sitting there saying, 'I don't know'. So we then had to take her to hospital, and we sat there till 4 am to be told, well if we admit her it won't have a good outcome so the best thing you can do is take her home and sleep with her until morning. And you really feel at a loss. You really do. You really feel at an absolute loss. It's so hard.

While Abigail spoke of her efforts to keep her daughter safe, Naomi shared this same dread for her son's safety, admitting that she had to move from a flat to a house because her anxiety of her son's suicidal threats was so acute. Naomi's fears in relation to her son's safety were so severe that it had very real material consequences for the family. To move home is a significant upheaval, and to do so in response to a perceived threat to the safety to your child highlights the seriousness of the distress she experienced:

And I said something has to give because we were in a flat before, and he used to threaten to jump out the window. It was soul destroying. I couldn't sleep in case I woke up and he was gone.

Scarlet became particularly distressed when discussing her fears for her daughter's future well-being, and her anxiety over potentially being unable to protect her from herself:

> For better or worse, I do remember being inside my head as a child, so I try to be the person I would have wanted. But it's depressing, frustrating … really seriously upsetting. And despite all of that, she still hurts herself. It's difficult seeing her go through it and not being able to help. Maybe I am helping, maybe it would have been worse, and she'd have gone through with her plans if I hadn't tried … you just want to be able to find a way to help her. And sometimes on a bad day, you feel like there just isn't. You feel helpless.

Her choice of language is powerfully emotive ('depressing', 'helpless') and conveys how all-consuming and distressing this particular lived experience is for mothers. The thought of losing a child is unthinkable, but to have your own child threaten to take themselves away is a viscerally distressing experience. I remember sitting in A&E with my son, at around age eight, who had begun to smash his head against the wall repeatedly following the death of my mother. After days of this, and days of him furiously sobbing that he no longer wanted to live, I didn't know what else to do. He was thankfully unhurt, not concussed or bearing any physical damage. As a result of his young age, the doctor, although well-meaning, dismissed the seriousness of my concern. I understood. What eight-year-old is serious about ending their life, one might ask? But yet, the nagging doubt that perhaps he might was utterly, bone-chillingly terrifying.

Mercifully, my son's experience of self-harm was short-lived. However, during his most challenging years he remained particularly violent, and such violence was directed almost exclusively towards me. He punched, he bit, he slapped, kicked, screamed, spat. These storms would appear, seemingly out of nowhere, and disappear almost as quickly sometimes, leaving me shaken and bewildered. The unpredictability of these outbursts left me in a state of hypervigilance, constantly aware of his presence and mood. I was quietly terrified of what would happen when his size eventually outmatched mine. Having previously left a relationship that had all too quickly become abusive, I found myself living in the same low-level state of anxiety, confusion and fear. At a particularly low moment, I sobbed to a friend that it felt almost like an abusive relationship that you could never leave. My husband found this period intensely difficult to witness. He felt powerless to intervene, and even if he did what could he do? Micah was only a child. He was not a grown man who knew the implications of his actions. He was my baby. After every outburst Micah would be devastated, seeking comfort from the very person he had wounded. The juxtaposition of these two 'Micahs' was profoundly traumatic.

However, since Asperger's bleak portrayal in 1944, research has increasingly refuted the association between aggression and malice described in individuals with autism. Patricia Howlin, in her guide for parents and practitioners of children with autism, considers that rather than 'aggression' there can be observed to be a 'perfect storm' of environmental and developmental factors that coalesce to create aggressive outbursts in autistic individuals. Difficulties in expressive language leading to communication difficulties and miscomprehension, sensory over-stimulation, or even under-stimulation leading to boredom and frustration, are increasingly considered to be causes of anger and aggression in individuals with autism-related conditions (Howlin and Asgharian, 1999, p. 211). As a means of de-stigmatizing such behaviours, in recent years a distinction has been drawn between 'tantrums' and the outbursts of extreme emotion exhibited by individuals with autism now popularly termed a 'meltdown'. The National Autistic Society describes a 'meltdown' as

... an intense response to overwhelming situations. It happens when someone becomes completely overwhelmed by their current situation and temporarily loses behavioural control. This loss of control can be expressed verbally (e.g. shouting, screaming, crying) physically (e.g. kicking, lashing out, biting) or in both ways.

Although extremely upsetting for both the individual themselves and the people around them, it is generally considered that such outbursts become less frequent as children get older (Howlin and Asgharian, 1999, p. 211). While it is uncertain whether children simply 'grow out' of such expressive outbursts, as typically developing children do with tantrums, it has been suggested that the acquisition of greater expressive language and increased awareness and avoidance of potential triggers, particularly environmental ones, can significantly reduce the frequency of meltdowns. It took us many months, and the intervention of a particularly perceptive occupational therapist, to discern the triggers that resulted in Micah becoming overwhelmed. While these triggers were often rooted in the seemingly mundane, everyday realities of daily living, being able to predict, pre-empt and ameliorate these everyday environmental triggers were crucial in being able to prevent some of his greatest struggles, and indeed my own.

And so the everyday emerges not simply as a site of struggle but, peculiarly, also a site of resistance. Michel de Certeau proposes that 'many everyday practices (talking, reading, moving about, shopping, cooking, etc.) are tactical in character', and that 'the wider social meanings to which we attach our experiences are rooted in the banalities of such seemingly unremarkable everyday tactics' (de Certeau, 1988, p. xix). In the next chapter, I will explore how the everyday becomes not solely the place in which struggles are felt and witnessed, but also where mothers become engaged in the creative practice of learning, adaptation and resistance.

Note

1 Children's support services are typically withdrawn once an individual reaches the age of 18.

'We will, of course, have him apologize to you. We do recognize the withdrawal of support has had an impact on Micah, which is deeply regrettable. You'll be pleased to know we have considered a support package appropriate to Micah's level of need.'

By this time, I was emboldened by our struggles. Furious and indignant.

'That is wonderful to hear. And I appreciate the offer of apology, which I will of course accept. However, what you fail to grasp is not only the effect it has on us in the present, but the impact it will have on the future. This "mistake" has withdrawn support that could have significantly impacted his life. We have lost ten months of progress. I also notice you state "Micah's need". I'm not sure what you consider Micah's needs to be; however, I assume from your choice of phrasing that my own do not factor?'

'Well...' she stuttered. 'It is Micah's support package. It's all about supporting him to be independent. We considered a respite allocation, but it was agreed that it would be of no significant benefit to Micah in terms of socialization or inclusion in the community.'

'Forgive me,' I interject, 'But the sign above the door says "Family Support", not "Child Support". Am I incorrect in assuming that you are duty bound to support families as a whole, and not just the child who is the subject of referral?'

'Well ... I mean ... yes, we are ... however, you must understand that we are at the mercy of the public purse. Funding decisions have to be made on a needs basis and in the best interests of the child. We always have to look first at what support family and friends can provide in our stead and perhaps this has been under-utilized...'

I did understand. I appreciated her predicament. Working within a charitable organization, the support I would like to offer is often tempered by the financial realities of what I am able to offer. That notwithstanding, I am also painfully aware of robbing Peter to pay Paul; cutting costs in support in the short term creates bigger social problems in the long term.

In the intervening ten months, out of our struggles, I had learnt to be creative with Micah's needs. Some of our old routines could be reinstated, others could be tweaked in such a way that it was still acceptable to him. Our tribe had rallied around us. My husband introduced him to the martial art of Muay Thai, finding an outlet for his anger, quelling his aggression and forging a bond out of a shared interest. To our eternal gratitude, his school had worked hard to support his inclusion, gradually increasing his participation and channelling his interests into the learning outcomes he needed to achieve. I enrolled him in swimming lessons, art classes. As a result of significant hard work, he was mercifully, eventually, coping. However, this delicate, intricate balance required constant thought, anticipation and effort. Every success was paid for with exhaustion.

'With respect. What YOU need to understand is that what you are offering Micah, I have already provided. His material needs are met, he is healthy. He is loved. He is included. He attends mainstream extra-curricular activities, independent of me. He has friends. I have done all that. WE have already done all of that. My son is without grandmothers, my father is 83 years old. My friends are scattered across the city and work full time. My partner works full time and doesn't live with us because Micah needs the consistency of our routine. They cannot, though they may want to, take on our day-to-day struggles. What we need from you is a recognition that while we mothers are killing ourselves to meet their needs, and killing ourselves to hide the fact that it is killing us, there is no one meeting OUR needs.'

15

Necessity is the Mother of Invention: 'Maternal Thinking' and Neglected Sites of Knowledge

The liberatory potential of the everyday has been developed by feminist theologians who critique traditional theologies neglect of 'the personal sphere' for its potential to shape and transform social, political and theological models (Isasi-Díaz, 2004, p. 67; Walton, 2014a, p. 9; Miller-McLemore, 1994, p. 142). Describing such everyday acts as 'tactics', de Certeau suggests further that even when we are engaged in practices that are seemingly routine and unconscious, we are often actively engaged in small but profoundly significant acts of resistance against dominant socio-political discourses (de Certeau, 1988, p. xvii).

De Certeau proposes that while seemingly unremarkable or habitual practices such as walking or the making of a meal have been discarded as trivial by analytic enquiry, they can in fact be shown to be poetic forms of making that demonstrate creativity and agency in the 'everyday struggles and pleasures' of our daily living (de Certeau, 1988, p. xx). Attention to the everyday, particularly the everyday lived maternal experience of a condition such as autism that so significantly and profoundly affects daily living, demands a recognition that life is messy. It is complex. It is shaped by social, political and theological debates that are interwoven into knots impossible to detangle. Theologies that attend to the liberatory potential of the 'everydayness' of struggle offer an important insight into the complexity of such lived experiences. Professor Heather Walton observes that:

Recognition has grown that the ofttimes neglected sphere of daily living is where most people exercise agency and construct selfhood. It is the plane on which our most meaningful life experiences unfold and also where the impact of economic and political forces are most keenly felt – and, in some cases, resisted. (Walton, 2020)

Developing this from a post-colonial feminist perspective, Ada Isasi-Díaz affirms the liberatory potential of lived experiences of everyday struggle as a vital theological source (2004). Critiquing dominant theological models that view struggle as a form of suffering, Isasi-Díaz develops a theological response that re-envisions struggle as an active, resistive way of living that she describes as '*en la lucha*' ('being in the struggle') (Isasi-Díaz, 2004, p. 229). In this sense, '*en la lucha*' instead 'represents a statement about survival, a comment on economic and social circumstances, a comment on coping and perseverance, and contains seeds of a commitment to be engaged, to be in struggle' (Schüssler-Fiorenza, 1996, p. 339). Central to Isasi-Díaz's theology of struggle is the concept of '*Lo cotidiano*'. While she utilizes this in various contexts to convey different meanings, '*Lo cotidiano*' broadly describes a process of active, ongoing participation in the choices, tactics and conversations (Latina) women engage in an everyday politics of resistance. It refers to the 'stuff' of Hispanic women's daily lives; their shared – but not common – choices, practices and understandings; complex, transitory and formed in the struggles of everyday life (Isasi-Díaz, 2004, p. 67). As Miller-McLemore asserts, 'we are most alive when passionately engaged in life's struggle, not when reflectively detached ... The academy does not usually understand this creative generative tension. A mother might' (Miller-McLemore, 1994, p. 142).

Mothers, by virtue of their conflicting demands, have had to develop ways of thinking and acting that are anticipatory and creative, immediately balancing the needs of the now with the consequences for the future. In the earlier chapters, I have described the everyday lived experiences of mothers whose struggles were particularly distinct. As a consequence of these distinct struggles, I have highlighted that mothers have had to become adept in adjusting to the needs of their children. This particular 'anticipatory' form of caring requires mothers to be creative, resourceful, flexible and resilient to the ever-changing and often circuitous needs of the child. Nicholas and colleagues observed that, following diagnosis, mothers of children on the spectrum often take on the role of 'researcher, advocate, and coordinator of services' for their children, immersing themselves in attempting to understand their child's condition and petitioning for appropriate support (Nicholas et al., 2016, p. 926).

Along with the other mothers who shared their experiences, I reflected on the significant amount of time we spent researching autism, both pre- and post-diagnosis, in an attempt to understand our children. As I have stressed, autism research is often conflicting, confusing, and little help to the specificity of any one particular child, yet it has provided us with the basis of knowledge to allow us to begin to act. Often, this required the painstaking documentation of the minutiae of daily living: our habits, routines, which particular noises, smells, textures could be discerned to accompany changes in our child's behaviour. As I have shared, this time and knowledge proved to be invaluable in ascertaining the everyday triggers that proved so challenging for Micah.

Once I understood that it was not the going to school that provoked such anxiety and fury in him, but rather putting his shoes on to leave the house, I was able to begin the process of trial and error in providing him with a solution – even if that solution was, in his case, a pair of all-weather sandals. I sewed belt loops on to jogging bottoms, I purchased compression sleeves, tight base layers that could be discreetly hidden under a uniform. Micah's room was transformed by a 'sensory tent', a place he could retreat to when overwhelmed, which I filled with fidget toys, bean bags, softly changing lights. Scarlet and Abigail similarly created 'sensory packs' for their children to carry with them, filled with Theraputty, tangle toys and even glow sticks. In learning our children's challenges, we began the work of orienting our lives around theirs – constructing routines, visual timetables, remembering the need to prepare – then re-prepare – our children for any deviation from their daily 'norm'.

This type of adaptation might well be considered to fall under the parameters of Macaskill's model of 'accommodative love' discussed in Chapter 12. However, I find that such a model implies a passivity in our acceptance of our children's additional caring needs, a 'working around' such everyday challenges. But as Nicholas and colleagues (2016) noted (highlighted in Chapter 14), the needs of our children were not merely 'accommodated', but rather they pervasively and unrelentingly shaped our thinking. Rather than 'accommodative love', I suggest that mothers of children on the spectrum demonstrate a distinctly heightened form of what Sara Ruddick terms 'attentive love'. In *Maternal Thinking: Towards a Politics of Peace*, Ruddick defines 'attentive love' as 'keeping over acquiring, of conserving the fragile, of maintaining whatever is at hand and necessary to the child's life, a loving without seizing or using that is akin to divine love for human creation' (Ruddick, 1990, p. 121).

The variously creative and pre-emptive tactics that mothers of children with autism can be seen to employ in efforts to maintain our children's well-being demonstrate precisely the kind of anticipatory and adaptive thinking that Ruddick outlines. She furthers that rather than self-sacrificial love, what is in fact distinct about mothers is that they possess a unique and generative way of thinking that has the potential to offer a very real and profound insight with regard to socio-political issues (Ruddick, 1990, p. 20). In this sense I propose that mothers, much as is assumed for those on the spectrum, think differently. Such insight also has the unique potential to reshape social visions.

However, I have described how the women I spoke with felt very strongly that their thoughts and value as mothers were respectively ignored, neglected or discounted by the professionals tasked with supporting them. Despite mothers' intimate knowledge of and creative engagement with their children's needs being the best source of 'raw data' that practitioners could utilize during diagnostic and intervention processes – and would arguably function to speed up and simplify processes that are currently arduous, complex and protracted – sadly, Kanner's legacy lives on, and there often remains a distinct disconnect between the contribution of the parent and the perceived authority of professionals in assessing diagnosis and providing support (Claiborne Park, 2002, p. 179). Heather Walton cautions that:

> While a romance still exists as to the nature of maternal care it will be impossible to address the dilemmas women face ... To recognise that these uneasy, painful relations are ones in which powerful emotional force is located is to begin to understand that they are possible sites from which to engage in the project of political transformation. (Walton, 2001, p. 9)

The strategies and tactics demonstrated above, while everyday in practice and nature, are thus often also tacitly employed in provoking 'resistance' to institutional barriers to support provision that do not accommodate our children's various, and varying, needs. Abigail reflected that while her daughter's school often identified problems in her child's learning, it was up to her to come up with the solutions. Scarlet shared similarly that with each new academic year, and subsequently each new teacher, she had to continually advocate for her daughter's individualized learning plan. While my son's school recognized the collaborative potential in engaging with my knowledge as his mother, as I outlined in this chapter's reflection, social support in the wider community was significantly more difficult to access. Such resistance required me to advocate, co-ordinate – and, in most cases, supplement – my son's support with independent resources.

Anne McGuire raises deep concerns in respect to narratives of parental advocacy, which, she highlights, are often more directly concerned with advocating for the needs of the parents, and not the child. There is an underlying, but implicit, anger in the tones in which she describes autism as something parents 'cope with'. This perspective challenges me in both a professional and a deeply personal way: as an academic, I can readily understand how discourses of power are interwoven in considering autism as something that affects the family, rather than the individual alone, or that indeed it is something that should be described as 'affecting' individuals at all.

However, as a mother of a child with autism, my gauge of myself has often, and as a direct consequence of my relationship to autism, been polarized into periods of 'coping' and 'not coping'. This is not to say that I believe autism to be inherently terrible – quite the contrary – but rather it is an honest admission that autism presents distinct challenges, for reasons both embodied and socially constructed, for those who live with it. I would counter this by saying that rather than advocating for support arising *from* our children's challenges, maternal advocacy instead recognizes the danger of 'pouring from an empty cup':

> As most families are set up, it will be the mother who does most of the considering, and one of the things she must consider is how much she can stand. It may be a great deal, but she must not take on everything in a misguided spirit of self-sacrifice, since if she cracks no one will be helped at all. (Claiborne Park, 1995, p. 114)

Rather than approaching the everyday and institutional struggles as problems to be solved, I suggest instead that mothers are able to maintain this intense and immersive level of care by being realistic about which challenges can be met and overcome, and which ones require a pragmatic approach. During a time when my own attempts at adaptation seemed like a very unsuccessful process of trial and error, I was advised to 'choose your battles'. While this may seem like an empty platitude, it has stuck with me in times of intense frustration and self-doubt. In three words, this sentence conveys that some difficulties may never be fully ameliorated; rather, we must pour what energy we do have into battles we know we can win. The theme of 'battle' has emerged recurrently through the mothers' stories in this book, and has illustrated that what is often defined as 'coping' is in fact an active, resistive and liberatory process for mothers navigating their children's autism. Scarlet commented:

> I fight in other ways. I fight on paper. I use my words. That fight ... gives me something to focus on. I write a complaint and I follow it like a dog with a bone ... I go on missions and if I run out of things to fight for for myself, I fight for other people. If someone has an issue I'm like, right, I'll sort this out! I keep myself busy, I never have a day where I don't have a dozen things to achieve and that's how I get through. I keep myself busy and I give myself fights to achieve and little things that I can win.

In this sense, while the distinct forms of maternal practice outlined above can arguably be described as forms of 'struggle' in a woman's daily life and thoughts, mothers can also be shown to draw significant strength from, and uniquely respond to, these struggles in a way that is distinctly productive and meaning-making. King and colleagues suggest that literature relating to parenting those with childhood disabilities has to date focused on a narrow model in which the child is seen to be the stressor, negating the possibility that parents may regard their experience as positive (King et al., 2006, p. 1076). Nicholas and colleagues further that for some of their participants, the challenges of their child's autism became 'purpose defining' within their lives (Nicholas et al., 2016, p. 929). Scarlet's account above highlights how important this sense of purpose is, both in terms of maternal self-perception and in ensuring positive outcomes for our children. Abigail, reflecting on her experience of motherhood in the context of her wider life experiences, suggested:

> I know you don't get time, but when you do get time it's good to think about yourself the way you were before you had children, and the way you've had to change yourself for their needs, and you realize, actually I'm a better person for this ... I absolutely know 100 per cent that I am a better person for

having those two children. I am a better person for having those two children with different needs that I need to think about and accommodate. I'm a much better person for it.

Abigail felt very strongly that her experience as a mother had not only changed her personally but had shaped her vocation. Her experiences with her children very much informed her practice, and positively so. In many ways, my participants considered themselves to have been made a 'better person' as a consequence of their child's autism, in their awareness and understanding of others and in the compassion and patience they found themselves capable of possessing (Nicholas et al., 2016, p. 929). In being able to overcome some of the challenges they faced or, as Claiborne Park articulates, discovering just how much one can bear, the mothers I spoke with reported a validation of their personal strength as a consequence of their experience.

Abigail's assertion was profoundly moving, and gave me pause to reflect on my own self-perception as a mother. In heeding Abigail's advice, and finding the time to reflect on these journeys, it is clear that my life has similarly changed direction following my son's diagnosis. While the delicate balance of mothering, work, research and life often felt impossible to negotiate, I wonder if I would have had the resilience to persevere without having adapted to this particular threshold of endurance. Without the experiences I had with my son, I would arguably have been unqualified, and emotionally ill-equipped, to manage my concurrent, and often conflicting, roles. I don't deny that the feelings of sadness, frustration and loneliness can be overwhelming at times, but slowly and over time they can become peripheral to a sense of accomplishment and strength that mothers may feel when, as Abigail suggests, we think about what used to be.

In the preceding two chapters, while the experiences articulated are all distinct, parallels can be drawn from Isasi-Díaz's notion of 'shared but not common' experience and the lived experience of the mothers interviewed (2004, p. 142). This holds particular resonance for the lives of mothers who are waging daily battles to obtain social support, fair healthcare outcomes, and inclusive education for their autistic children – and yet also battling the inconsistency and relentlessness of a daily life shaped by sensory overloads and disrupted sleep patterns. I have noted that while the unusual challenges of our children's daily routines and habits can be a significant source of struggle, mothers of children on the spectrum often develop creative ways of engaging with this struggle that resist the potential for becoming overwhelmed. Many of the struggles that emerged from mothers who outlined their experiences in this book can be seen to be shared, yet were experienced and resisted in different ways.

It must be noted, though, that Isasi-Díaz's theology of '*lo cotidiano*' was developed in response to the particularities of the struggles of Hispanic women. Kwok Pui-lan questions whether, by focusing on these Hispanic women, Isasi-Díaz's insights can really be translated to other contexts (Kwok Pui-lan, 2011, p. 35). This raises an important point. Although Isasi-Díaz, as a Cuban-American woman, situates herself within her own particular research context, her reflections highlight that even within a perceived 'community' the experiences of those within that community may be more unequal than equal. Womanist and liberation theologians such as Ada Isasi-Díaz, Nancy Eiesland, and Marcella Althaus-Reid have utilized their distinct academic advantage, in being outside a white, heterosexual or able-bodied male experience, to give voice to women of colour, individuals with disabilities, and those who are marginalized and oppressed by dominant social orders. Goto observes that in this way feminist theologies subvert our perceptions – de-familiarizing what we assume we know to be familiar (for example, the lives of mothers) while making familiar the lives of those who are perceived to be different from our own. She cautions, though, that 'as feminist theology slowly transforms awareness, what once needed translation can become assimilated by the dominant discourse' (Goto, 2018, p. 67). In this sense, we must be wary of the 'conceptual trap of "solidarity"' in assuming a universal, hegemonic (and usually white) category of women whose experiences and struggles are easily transferrable with others. It can be all too easy 'to fall prey to this', and to neglect our own positions of privilege and power in representing the voices of other women (Althaus-Reid, 2000, p. 90).

I am a white woman, who has been educated within a white, middle-class, predominantly Christian, academic setting. My research is being conducted in the west of Scotland, which is a similarly largely white, Christian demographic. Research that investigates the experience of autism in BAME[1] communities is limited; however, a 2014 study by the National Autistic Society suggests that diagnosis and access to support may be significantly more difficult for individuals who are non-white: this is as a consequence of potential language difficulties, access to resources, or indeed biases from professionals themselves.[2] My book therefore reflects a predominantly white lived experience, and does not investigate the ways in which racial inequalities may significantly impact this experience. This theological reflection has not been intended to be an exhaustive analysis of these many different perspectives; rather, it is but one perspective in a complex issue.

Consequently, I am cautious of the potential dangers of making assumptions about the experiences of others to suit methodological ends (Goto, 2018, p. 28). I recognize the problems involved in speaking of experiences that are similar to my own, yet also not my own. In responding to Isasi-Díaz, Kwok asks, how can we, as academics, authentically speak of the experiences of others, particularly when the voices of those others resist our theological scripts? (Kwok Pui-lan, 2011, p. 35).

While I came to this research with an understanding of many of the issues that might emerge, my knowledge of these issues could not assume exactly *what* they might reveal. My participants were similar to me in many ways, speaking of struggles I knew all too well. However, their experiences were also distinct from my own in many ways. One such way was that they all had more than one child. This does not, of itself, appear very significant. Nor did it to me. However, in considering my own experience, and questioning what might be different about the voices I seek to represent, it became particularly meaningful.

In reflecting on their shared stories, it was evident that certain aspects of their motherhood experience differed considerably between their children. The differences were often subtle; however, it was clear that mothering a child with autism involved considerably more time demands, thought, physical effort and financial consequences. What has been a revelation to me is that I myself had until recently (and admittedly naively) considered the daily struggles I experienced as rooted in the experience of mothering generally, rather than specifically mothering a child with autism. In reflecting on these subtle yet significant differences, I suggest that while mothering children with autism embodies the many aspects of maternal struggle I have explored in this chapter, these challenges are *magnified* by their relationship to autism. This positions the experience of mothering a child on the autism spectrum as a distinctly amplified and intense form of maternal struggle, and one that is not given attention within current theologies of motherhood.

Viewed against the backdrop of material inequality and social policies that fail to respond to our pressing need for services, it would have been tempting to situate this book within a liberationist theological position. Liberation theologies, as I have stated, offer a particular resistance to oppression. My participants in this book, and I suppose myself, actively participate in acts of resistive and liberatory practices every day. These women are advocates, researchers, campaigners, educators. They are arguably making more strides in liberatory practices in the everyday realities of negotiating their children's curriculum, and access to activities, clubs and churches within their community, than my academic exercise in presenting their stories could ever hope to achieve. At the same time, these efforts are approached with a heavy measure of pragmatism. We are winning small battles for own children, sharing battle tactics and knowledge so that other children may benefit. However, the large-scale structures that shape and contribute to our struggles are so complex and over-arching at a societal level that it would be naïve and idealistic to believe that we are likely to see considerable, meaningful change within the fleetingly short span of our children's childhoods. Therefore, our experiences cannot simply be reduced to that of socio-political marginalization. These social forces have undoubtedly shaped our experience of struggle, yet we were also profoundly affected by our daily realities of mothering, in the unrelenting 'little stuff' that we know will re-start, cyclically and cease-lessly, day after day.

Summary

In this section, I have critiqued the reluctance of theology to fully engage with mothers as an important and generative source of theological reflection, articulating an experience of mother-hood that defies incorporation into the dominant ideological paradigms of 'traditional motherhood'. I have considered how theologies that focus on issues of struggle in everyday contexts can speak to the experience of mothers whose lives are shaped by struggles that are disregarded as seemingly mundane and unremarkable, yet that significantly inform their choices, prac-tices and experiences of living. What is particular about the lived experiences that have emerged in this research is that they are doubly constrained by both dominant debates concerning disability and dominant discourses of motherhood, and yet do not fit neatly within either. In the same way that I have consid-ered how theologies of disability have neglected the experience of mothers, so too have theologies of motherhood and struggle not fully attended to the added complexity of motherhood in relation to disability.

Our lived experiences are thus revealed to be theologically problematic, as they cannot be adequately reconciled within any one theological model. A theological response that attends to the particularity and distinctness of such experiences must be similarly particular and distinct, resisting the temptation to neatly round off the edges of what is revealed to fit within the boundaries of what has already been written. In the following concluding chapter, I will draw together theological elements that hint at this particular experience, from those proposing a theological response that attends to the complexity and ongoingness of lived experiences that are simultaneously ambiguous and mundane, resisted yet unresolved.

Notes

1 'BAME' is an acronym used to refer to 'Black, Asian and Minority Ethnic' communities. It has become increasingly used in discussions relating to socio-political inequalities, but it is worth noting that its usage is contested, with some considering the amalgamation of these distinct communal identities arbitrary. See Nora Fakim and Cecilia Macauley (2020), '"Don't Call Me BAME": Why Some People Are Rejecting the Term', 30 June, *BBC News*, www.bbc.co.uk/news/amp/uk-53194376, accessed 17.07.20.

2 See www.autismvoice.org.uk/wp-content/uploads/2018/03/AUTISM-IN-THE-BAME-COMMUNITY-UK-ISSUE-PAPER.pdf, accessed 17.07.20.

'Mum.'

'Yes, baby?'

'Why is that on the wall?'

The 'that' he was referring to was quite a large representation of Christ on the cross. It was situated on the landing of the stairway we were currently climbing, with each step seemingly bringing us closer to him. We were in St Margaret's Hospice, visiting my mother on the palliative care ward. Everywhere, there were subtle nods to the religious tradition in which the hospice stood; however, this was perhaps the most striking example.

I contemplated my response. This is a complicated question, but I attempt a simple answer.

'That's Jesus, baby…'

He was patient with me. 'I know that, Mum. What I mean is, why do they want us to see him like that? I don't know if it's good for the patients to be reminded of being in pain like that.'

He is concerned. I understand his reservation. He firmly believes in distraction as the best form of medicine. To see such a visual representation of suffering, surely, must be counter-productive to 'feeling better'.

'That's a very good question, baby. Yes, he is in pain. But they have that there to remind us that even Jesus suffers. That sometimes helps people feel a bit less frightened when they're poorly or in pain.'

'It IS a bit scary though, isn't it?'

'I suppose it is, baby…'

He is quiet for a few seconds. He is struggling with some big questions at the moment, I know. Why is his Nanny sick, why can the doctors not make her better. When can she come home. It is difficult for him to be here, to be unable to avoid the realities of sickness and suffering he faces on the ward and have no answers for *why they exist. Not knowing is a difficult thing for any-one, but for someone with autism the concept that there can be a question without an answer is unbearably so.*

He has truly humbled me in his ability to be present for his grandmother in the absence of answers. The sadness that I cannot shield him from the pain and confusion of this period, however, has become a heavy ache in my bones.

'Mum,' he says again, finally. I steel myself for more difficult questions.

'Do you think they'll have the good biscuits today?'

I smile, relieved.

'If they know what's good for them,' I wink. The big questions can wait for another day. Today, it is enough that they have the good biscuits.

16

Lived Experience in Practical Theology: Knowing Your Limits

> Practical theology wants to keep our relationship with the world so that we are never quite 'done' with things; rather, always undoing and redoing them, so that we can keep the 'doing' happening – passionate, keen, expectant – never satisfied, never quite finished. (Veling, 2005, p. 7)

This book has sought to develop an understanding of autism as a deeply ambiguous, misunderstood condition, resistant to disciplinary categorization. I have shown that autism occupies a position of incongruence in that it can be seen to be strongly shaped by dominant debates on disability, and yet is 'invisible' and 'dis-embodied' in ways that disability theory largely neglects. Autism is thus 'unresolved' in many ways. Its cause is unclear; and an individual's symptoms can be seen to change, improve or regress in unpredictable ways. Therefore, what we know and understand about autism is continually evolving. What has emerged from the sharing of our stories is that mothering a child on the spectrum is an experience that is similarly complex and distinct – and largely theologically sidelined. Our children's needs are varied and conflicting, often hidden within the seemingly unremarkable events of daily life. Facing these challenges in silence, we have had little opportunity to speak of our experiences.

While I entered this research with an awareness that what I might find could 'render my world stranger' (Bennett et al., 2018, p. 143), I perhaps naively anticipated that our accounts would, nonetheless, echo much of what has been written and find their theological home. However, as Goto and Kwok have reminded us, lived experiences, even when assumed to be common, are subjective and so resistant to generalization (Goto, 2018, p. 29; Kwok Pui-lan, 2011, p. 35). In the last chapter, I raised the question of how practical theology may respond to lived experiences that 'unsettle our theological assumptions'. Goto suggests that our compulsion to answer this question, to generalize or categorize experiences to fit an expected outcome, is at the root of a fundamental problem in the way practical theology constructs knowledge (Goto, 2018, p. 222).

In attempting to reconcile our findings within traditional 'conceptual frameworks', Goto proposes that we inhibit our own ability to generate new knowledge, and instead preserve what is already assumed to be known. What is 'already known' in practical theology, Tom Beaudoin suggests, is shaped by an unconscious and unquestioned white, male 'christianicity' that forms the theological blueprint for our practices, knowledge and interpretations (Beaudoin, 2016, p. 18). In his deconstruction of the 'practices' of practical theology, Beaudoin reveals formulaic processes at work that he suggests unconsciously shape what we consider to be 'theological':

> ... an intervention is normally framed in a theologically naturalized or essentialised fashion, such as claims about God-material showing itself in, through, or in relation to practice, along these familiar lines; God cares about X, Jesus is concerned with Y, the Spirit is known through Z. (Beaudoin, 2016, p. 16)

This formula suggests a coherence and orderliness in which practice and theory are unproblematically reconciled. However, the reality, as we know, is much more complex.

Approaching these tensions from a feminist, post-colonial perspective, Marcella Althaus-Reid has been particularly vocal in her critique that practical theology has been constructed in ways that determine exactly whose experiences count as theologically significant (Althaus-Reid, 2000, p. 18). As a female practical theologian who is 'outside' of a faith tradition, I have all too often felt a seductive pressure to situate my writing in relation to what has gone before, to speak in a 'Christian' voice that is not necessarily my own in order to legitimize what I am saying. My participants themselves all had distinctly different attitudes to faith and relationships with the divine. Some, indeed, had none. If I had attempted to reconcile their voices within established theological boundaries, would this have excluded them from even entering the discussion?

Heather Walton considers that these issues raise fundamental questions as to 'whether practical theologians possess the capability to engage with voices that resist incorporation into conventional frames of academic credibility and coherence' (Walton, 2018, p. 10). As someone whose voice resists such conventional frames, the question 'But am I really a theologian?' has plagued me throughout this research. Frustrated by the gaps and silences I encountered when attempting to locate our experience theologically, the gnawing doubt crept in. 'If theology does not speak to this experience, is it even really theological?'

Drawing on Beaudoin's work in *Conundrums in Practical Theology* (2016), Walton suggests that it is indeed right that we should question what is 'theological' about our work. However, she proposes that perhaps the gnawing anxiety this question provokes stems not from our own academic insecurities, but rather from a deeply hidden awareness that how we measure what is 'theological' is itself what is arguably problematic (Walton, 2014b, p. 226). She suggests that perhaps the answer is, 'We have never been theologians' (p. 224). This provocative declaration is not intended to be a sweeping rejection of the work of theology, but rather an invitation to challenge our deeply held beliefs over what our task as theologians really is.

Increasingly, practical theology is being challenged to adopt more diverse, interdisciplinary models of theological reflection. In a pluralistic globalized society, Walton proposes that instead of lingering within the nostalgic comfort of tradition, we ought to reconsider how practical theology can creatively respond to the ambivalence and ambiguity of our post-secular world (Walton, 2018, p. 226). Developing this from a feminist perspective, Elaine Graham has offered nuanced and sophisticated contributions on the challenges of post-secularism and post-humanism within practical theology; this urges us to find creative and engaging ways of moving between the 'rocks and hard places' of what we think we know, and what is really in front of us (Graham, 2013, p. 60). Challenging us to become more comfortable with blurred boundaries and theological ambiguities, she reminds us that 'difference serves as disclosive, in that a deeper and larger truth is revealed as resting in diversity and pluriformity' (p. 200).

Beaudoin affirms that practical theology must therefore 'hold open pre-Christian, Christian, post-Christian, and non-Christian meanings all at once, and let those meanings be non-exclusive to each other' (Beaudoin, 2016, p. 28). Considering what this may mean for the discipline, he asks, 'Is practical theology left with empty hands? No – or rather, Yes: practical theology is left with hands that become theological by how they give away what was never the property of Christianity to begin with' (p. 28). This is not to suggest that practical theology ought to 'throw the baby Jesus out with the bath water'. Tradition is important. Rather, what the work of Beaudoin, Walton and Graham highlight is that practical theologians should now take the opportunity to critically examine our own preconceptions of knowledge, defamiliarizing what we presume to be theology and pushing us towards new and diverse ways of knowing.

In earlier chapters, I explored many different theological responses when considering how I may come to locate and draw meaning from this particular maternal experience. These theologies are all distinct; however, I would argue that they largely share a common thread in that what we are offered are theological reconciliations, whether their aims are at the personal level of accepting love (Swinton, 2012c; Macaskill, 2019; Reynolds, 2008) or at the social level of effecting change (Eiesland, 1994; Block, 2002; Isasi-Díaz, 2011). In the theologies explored, what can arguably be demonstrated is a thread of 'overcoming'. Yet, as I have sought to highlight, our stories defied the archetypal narrative pattern of 'beginning, conflict, and resolution' (Atkinson, 1998, p. 3; Walton, 2018, p. 2). The concept of 'overcoming' thus offers little value to an experience of motherhood that is rooted in the ongoing daily realities of struggle, challenge, grief and joy from which there is no overcoming. I argue that in fact the suggestion of overcoming is potentially harmful, as it implies an end point to struggle that for some never comes.

Lifelong developmental conditions (such as we could describe autism) thus present as particularly problematic, as they do not fit with the expectation that struggle is temporary. It is quite one thing, Hauerwas asserts, to be present and sympathetic with someone who is suffering for a few days or a few weeks; it is quite another to 'be compassionate year in and year out' (Hauerwas, 2005, p. 550). While I would not go so far as to say that living with autism could be described as 'suffering', I suggest that the maternal response to autism requires exactly what Hauerwas suggests is unmanageable. The maternal experience of autism is distinctly challenging for precisely this reason; it requires a level of attentive care that is compassionate, ongoing and unending.

I have articulated the continuousness and pervasiveness of the characteristics of autism in disrupting the seemingly mundane and taken-for-granted social scripts and activities of everyday life. I have described how everyday care demands, anticipatory planning and unknowns of what the future may hold presented as particularly traumatic and exhausting for mothers of children on the spectrum. While I examined the idea that such complex feelings could be considered within the context of 'grief', both in terms of loss of one's own independence and loss of one's aspirations for our children, I argued that current models of grief, and parental grief, were often unhelpfully framed within the context of restoration.

In the context of disability, there is the inherent danger of relying on models of suffering that assert its potential to be morally transformative or beneficial to personal growth. In so doing, we perpetuate a discourse in which we believe it should have a point, or a cure, and allow ourselves to deny the fact that suffering simply is. As I showed in the last chapter, such struggle, and indeed suffering, cannot be reduced to a temporary challenge but is rather ongoing and rooted in the particularities of everyday living. Mothers' ability to navigate the continuousness and relentlessness of caregiving demands did not depend on their or their child's restoration to a peaceable 'whole', but rather on the ability to adopt a pragmatic acceptance, both of their own children's limits and capabilities, and of their own limits in what they are able to shoulder.

In considering my participants' struggle, I too fell into the trap of attempting to locate the 'how' in their survival. How did they cope, how did they make sense of the struggle, how did they find meaning in their experiences? I myself have been asked this question many times. I have often been left wordless in response, and at other times frustrated by its naiveté. The simple answer to this was, we just did. My subjects and I are all distinct. Some of us acknowledge relationships with the divine, others do not. Yes, we spoke about our experiences having made us better people, and they have doubtless provided a different perspective on life. Yet the ways in which we considered this transformation or the meanings we attached to it were all very different. While some possessed a belief in the revelatory power of their experience, others were merely trying to get through the day. This was our life, there was little choice. As our shared accounts have highlighted, there is often little opportunity for respite.

While I have sought to demonstrate that while this particular maternal experience has been shown to be strongly shaped by socio-political policies from above, the daily challenges of everyday living are also so all-encompassing that we must carefully 'choose our battles' in deciding exactly which struggle takes precedence. In being faced with such a choice, one or more battles are necessarily and inevitably lost. Our stories have reflected an active, ongoing resistance against institutional barriers to our children's well-being, yet also admitted a weariness in acknowledging that our potential to ever fully overcome these is limited. Thus, our 'tactics of resistance' are enacted with an acceptance that they are unlikely to solve all of our challenges; rather, they may ameliorate them just enough to fortify us for the next battle to be waged.

Drawing from Bonnie Miller-McLemore (1994, p. 142) and Sara Ruddick (1990, p. 20), I have situated this pragmatic adaptability as a distinctly active, anticipatory and resilient form of 'maternal thinking' that has significant generative potential for engaging with alternative stories of motherhood. Challenging the relegation of motherhood and its challenges to the 'domestic sphere', I have proposed that the everyday tactics of attentive mothering I have described are instead creative sites of resistance against the absence of institutional support. In attending to the conflict of struggles from both 'above' and 'below', I have considered the work of Isasi-Díaz (2002; 2014) and de Certeau (1988) as particularly constructive in illuminating the tension between the political and the personal in our daily lives. Walton, drawing from de Certeau, proposes that attention to the everyday reveals the unnameable and unknowable in our encounter with the other, in a way that opens us up to the disruptive possibility of transformation (Walton, 2014b, p. 184). In reminding us that the 'everyday' is not a site of passive acceptance or mundane banality, but rather that some of our deepest theological challenges can be found within the mundane, messy complexity of everyday moments, these theologies acknowledge the liberatory potential of the everyday as a site of struggle and resistance.

I have expressed my deeply held reluctance, however, to disingenuously represent our experiences within a context of 'liberation'. Liberation implies a release from the *sources* of struggle, which, in this particular lived experience, is not only unrealistic, but is in many ways impossible. Autism is a lifelong developmental condition. Many of the struggles we as mothers face have been shown to be directly related to the symptoms of autism that, as I have highlighted, may improve, but will never disappear. In a similar way, while the organizational and attitudinal sources of struggle we experience may be resisted, they are so overarching that we often simply do not have the time, resources or energy to overcome them.

Recent work by Nicola Slee has highlighted the potential to

become over-burdened by everyday 'multiple overwhelmings' that are complex, overlapping and multi-faceted, yet also an inescapable part of life (Slee, 2017, p. 21). Drawing on Deborah Creamer's theology of limits as a natural, unremarkable part of living, Slee considers a theological re-framing of 'overwhelmings' and struggle as normative, rather than counter-intuitive, to our daily lives (p. 26). In the context of autism as a lifelong developmental condition, then, models of restoration do not apply to the lived experience of autism as a condition that is lifelong, and thus whose struggles and challenges are ongoing.

Shelley Rambo, in her work on trauma, proposes that theodicies that imply restoration or resolution from trauma neglect the cyclical, ongoing and enduring nature of struggles that are 'lived with' and 'without end' (Rambo, 2010, p. 15). Rambo's work can be seen to offer potential release from the oppressive structures of tradition explored above that neglect the 'ongoingness' and 'everydayness' of suffering as simply part of our normal human lives. Describing her work on trauma as 'suffering which does not go away', Rambo instead invites us to find 'resonance in the unknowing', resisting the urge to find theological justifications for experiences that are uncomfortable, unsettling and unspeakable (Rambo, 2010, p. 15).

Arguably, we are all guilty of attempting to find reasons and justifications for our experiences. Acceptance of human limits as advocated by Creamer and Rambo thus challenges the enduring and damaging theological approaches that consider suffering as some form of divine punishment. I found myself profoundly moved when Abigail reflected on one particularly difficult moment, in which her son questioned why God made him autistic. This reminded me of a tearful conversation in which I asked my mother a similar question: 'Is he being punished because of me? Am I being punished? Why us?' My mother, who understood such struggles and questions, replied, 'My darling, God knows what we can handle. And he knew that you are the only person in the world who could handle him.' Abigail responded to her son with similarly tender pragmatism, 'Because, Son, God has put you with a family that he knows can support you. Somebody in this world has got to have autism, sweetheart, so it might as well be someone who can be supported and loved through it.' These insightful women unwittingly affirmed Rambo's and Creamer's position that while there is no answer to the question of suffering, we can address this within a perspective that takes cognizance of human, and also divine, potentialities and limits.

Theologies that acknowledge our human limits, and the often theologically irreconcilable nature of struggle and suffering as part of our human experience, arguably offer a more holistic and realistic model of inclusion than the models of disability explored previously. Rather than thinking of limits solely in a negative sense (what we, or what God, cannot do), this perspective offers alternatives for thinking about boundaries and possibilities. In an age of war, terrorism, economic injustice and environmental risk, a recognition and theological affirmation of limits seems more responsible than apathy or omnipotent control and offers a perspective that can lead to hopeful possibilities of perseverance, strength, creativity and honest engagement with the self and the other (Creamer, 2009, p. 113).

I am thus drawn towards a theology that offers a recognition that autism 'is what it is' and not some divine form of punishment or moral challenge to learn through difficulty. In the preceding chapter, I articulated that such acceptance is crucial to a mother's ability to cope with and respond to the challenges of their lived experience. Instead of looking to faith to provide explanations or solutions, such an approach suggests that perhaps God rather gifts us with the theological wisdom we need to deal with the suffering and unresolvedness that comes from being human. Acknowledgement of our 'limits' not only speaks to the practical acceptance of what we cannot change but also defies the dominant theological imperative to seek resolutions. This acknowledgement does not assume that all struggles can easily be made sense of, nor should they be, but rather invites us to endure: creatively, actively, pragmatically, in the midst of, and in spite of, our struggle. In acknowledging the limits of both our personhood and of the divine, such a perspective opens up the potential for more fluid and diverse modes of theological reflection, reframing our relationship to God in a way that 'not only offers corrective guidelines to established theologies but also itself raises new theological possibilities' (Creamer, 2009, p. 78).

Unprecedented.
  Uncertain.
  Socially distant.
  These are the watchwords that are defining our 'new normal', as it has come to be called. There is nothing normal about it, which, in a strange way for us, is almost comforting. We are used to making 'new normals'.

  In the final weeks of my writing, our world was rendered stranger than even we were used to. We had heard rumblings, murmurs, a foreshadowing of what was to come. Yet when it came, it felt sudden, abrupt, like jumping into cold water you expected to be warm. On the day of the announcement, Micah had a mere 12 weeks left of primary school. We had submitted a placing request to our high school of choice, and he was anxiously trying to stem back the flow of time until he would have to say goodbye to the faces, rooms and routines he once knew. As it would turn out, goodbyes were to come a lot sooner than expected. We were in 'lockdown'. In response to the catastrophic damage Covid-19 was wreaking across the globe, we were plunged into a state of suspended animation, urged to 'stay home to save lives'.

  On that last school day, I waited at the same spot I had every day for seven years, but it was different now. He was different now. No longer did I stand in dread, anxious of the day he had had. Our days have slowly, gradually, become, to all intents and purposes, something close to 'normal'. That last day was not to be one of those days. That last day, he came out of the main door. Flanked by his teachers, they formed a guard of honour, clapping as his class tearfully left school for what was likely to be the last time. At one time, his participation in this would have been unthinkable. That day I watched as he walked out shoulder to shoulder with his peers, fighting back tears, but a part of it all. We didn't know if they would be able to return. We knew simply that we had to mark this moment for them, to pre-empt a conclusion that was yet to be drawn.

It has now been 10 weeks since that day. There have now been over 400,000 deaths worldwide. Our 'new normal' is composed of oxymorons: 'self-isolation', 'socially distant', 'working from home'. All of our carefully calibrated equilibriums have been thrown into disarray. Our routines, disordered. Our social supports, severed.

With all the unknown, and in the absence of the comforting and reliable structure school provided, many of the issues we had thought were things of the past have resurfaced. The 'tics' that we had believed to have disappeared years ago are now a regular occurrence. Micah's anxieties are manifesting in the 'little things' he can exert control over; once again, shoes are his nemesis. My days are spent anxiously trying to pre-empt these challenges, trying (often futilely) to create some sense of order to his little world. In between these attempts, I am working from home, writing, teaching ... washing, cooking, comforting ... mothering. On some days, I have been able to balance these commitments; on others, I have been left hollow, exhausted from the effort.

And yet, there is a curious sense of calm in our imposed isolation. I have been able to re-learn who Micah is, to see him through my own eyes, and not the stares of others. We have very recently learned that, despite our fears, he will in fact be able to attend the school we had hoped for. I am acutely aware, however, that many of the carefully choreographed mechanisms that have sustained his ability to manage will not follow him there. Right now, we don't know what high school will look like when it comes. Will he continue to learn from home? Will I be able to return to work? We don't know what the world will look like. I don't know how he will cope with all the change, the uncertainty, the unknown. All I can hope for is that others will learn to enjoy Micah, and say, with unfeigned sincerity, 'I am glad you are here.'

Conclusion

'Pragmatic Unresolvement' – Towards a New Theology of Struggle

When I began my research for this book, I thought that its theological contribution would be to highlight a lived experience that was obscured, and difficult to name. I anticipated, though, that the stories presented would find their theological home within the words and pages of others who had chosen to share their lives. Instead, what has emerged is a theological response to the gaps and silences in those narratives, to the tensions and conflicts between what is considered known in practical theology and lived experiences that defy to be known.

In focusing on these experiences as an ongoing and distinctly difficult form of maternal struggle, I proposed an interdisciplinary theological response that recognizes that experiences are not singular or unrelated, but rooted in the overlapping and complex forces of daily life that do not easily make sense within any singular framework. I propose that what is currently absent, and what is needed, is a theology that attends to life as it is and does not attempt to silence experiences it cannot neatly explain within the accepted discourses available to it. In response, I offer a new theological thinking, drawing from the theological approaches that have almost touched, but not quite reached, the lived experience I have revealed in this book. I invite you as the reader to consider a theological response that acknowledges that life is often unsettled, unresolved, and that not all challenges can be quite so neatly tucked away.

Responding to the ambiguity of lived experiences whose edges are blurred and permeable, I propose a theology of what I will term 'pragmatic unresolvement'. In drawing together the threads of active, everyday maternal experiences revealed here, this theological response is *pragmatic* in proposing an acceptance of the cyclical, conflicting and irresolvable forms of struggle that lie outside our ability to conquer. This theological response is also *unresolved*, in that it recognizes the ongoing, cyclical and compounded nature of struggles that do not have a definitive end point, nor the potential for overcoming. Theologies that focus on the unsettled, the unknowable and the ambiguous may offer significant potential in challenging our deeply held assumptions about both our tasks as theologians, and our relationship to the divine. They may give space to reflect on experiences that are not temporal, immediately visible or easily understood.

Presenting us with the theological challenge to see and bear with the 'ongoingness' and 'unsettledness' of daily living, such a theology seeks to blur the boundaries between immanence and transcendence in a way that is fluid, adaptive and 'never quite done' (Veling, 2005, p. 7). In an age of ever-increasing uncertainty, of economic instability, political tensions and global health inequalities, it is even more important that we move beyond theological models that distinguish between Christian/non-Christian, divine omnipotence or secular abandonment, and 'consider this more risky, immanent and vulnerable image of a God who permits Godself to be caught up within the overwhelming' (Slee, 2017, p. 31). Reminding us that our tasks as theologians is to risk transformation, Walton revels in the complexity, ambiguity, chaos and wonder of life as it is, not as we expect to find it:

> I know I am most alive in the messy, compelling, tragi-passions of everyday life. I do not seek deliverance from them but rather revelations within them. In fact the thing I probably most fear is the resolution of contraries in a peaceable whole. The stark irresolutions we encounter (they make both beauty and tragedy) are what make us human, and for me these are also the key to understanding God in the light of incarnation. (Walton, 2014b, p. 86)

The emergence of this book was unanticipated but instinctive, responsive to the theological silences it encountered. In proposing a theology of 'pragmatic unresolvement', I do not presume to have offered a new, cohesive and complete methodological approach. Rather, in drawing from theologies of limits, I acknowledge that this theology too is limited. In undertaking research that looks to the experiences of mothers, I have admittedly excluded the voices of fathers, and indeed individuals with autism themselves. As I have touched upon in Chapter 15, this book also reflects a predominantly white lived experience, and does not investigate the ways in which racial inequalities may significantly impact this experience. My theological reflections do not intend to be an exhaustive analysis of these many different perspectives; rather, it is but one perspective of a complex issue. This is merely the beginning of a conversation, one that I invite you to continue. Therefore, it is the beginning of something that is not yet done. It is a call to invite others to consider wading into the murky waters of a theological engagement with life as unknowable, unsettled and thoroughly untameable.

Postscript: Micah's Own Words

Having autism doesn't necessarily mean that you are extremely hard to take care of or will always have trouble managing things. But I feel as though being diagnosed with autism is challenging, so it's a strange thought being different from other people. I also have Tourette's syndrome, which can be challenging because I have had multiple tics. ADHD is also a challenge. I take pills to limit my extra energy. It is sometimes difficult to take a pill every morning and night. Sometimes I forget to take it, but most of the time I remember.

I think I have grown so much from when I was younger. I went from being an aggressive kid with anger issues to one of the most relaxed people I know. I think that when I was younger it was probably very challenging for my mum, and it probably still is. But I think we have bonded so much throughout my life, it's extraordinary. I hope she thinks so too.

My darling Micah. I think so too.

Bibliography

Abberley, Paul (2002), 'Work, disabled people and European social theory' in C. Barnes, M. Oliver and L. Barton, *Disability Studies Today*, Cambridge: Polity Press.

Albrecht, Gloria (1995), *The Character of our Communities*, Nashville, TN: Abingdon Press.

Althaus-Reid, Marcella (2000), *Indecent Theology: Theological Perversions in Sex, Gender and Politics*, London: Routledge.

Anderson, Leon (2006), 'Analytic autoethnography', *Journal of Contemporary Ethnography*, 35(4), pp. 373–95.

Atkinson, Robert (1998), *The Life Story Interview*, London: Sage Publications.

Auyeung, Bonnie et al. (2009), 'Fetal testosterone and autistic traits', *British Journal of Psychology*, February, part 1, pp. 1–22.

Baird, Gillian et al. (2006), 'Prevalence of disorders of the autism spectrum in a population cohort of children in South Thames: the Special Needs and Autism Project (SNAP)', *Lancet*, 368, pp. 210–15.

Barnes, C., Oliver, M. and Barton, L. (2002), *Disability Studies Today*, Cambridge: Polity Press.

Baron-Cohen, Simon and Patrick Bolton (1993), *Autism: The Facts*, Oxford: Oxford University Press.

Baron-Cohen, Simon (2002), 'The extreme male brain theory of autism', *Trends in Cognitive Sciences*, 6(6), pp. 248–54.

Baron-Cohen, Simon, A. Leslie and U. Frith (1985), 'Does the autistic child have a theory of mind?', *Cognition*, 21, pp. 37–46.

Beaudoin, Tom (2016), 'Why does practice matter theologically?', in B. Miller-McLemore, *The Wiley-Blackwell Companion to Practical Theology*, Oxford: Blackwell.

Bennett, Zoë et al. (2018), *Invitation to Research in Practical Theology*, Abingdon and New York: Routledge.

Betcher, Sharon (2007), *Spirit and the Politics of Disablement*, Minneapolis, MN: Fortress Press (e-book, available from https://hdl.handle.net/2027/heb.30705).

Block, Jennie (2002), *Copious Hosting: A Theology of Access for People with Disabilities*, New York: Continuum.

Boff, Leonardo (1986), *Liberation Theology: From Dialogue to Confrontation*, Frisco, TX: Harper and Row.

Bons-Storm, Riet (1996), *The Incredible Woman: Listening to Women's Silences in Pastoral Care and Counseling*, Nashville, TN: Abingdon Press.

Bowlby, John (1960), 'Grief and mourning in infancy and early childhood', *The Psychoanalytic Study of the Child*, 15, pp. 9–52.

Bristol Marie M., J. J. Gallagher and K. D. Holt (1993), 'Maternal depressive symptoms in autism: response to psychoeducational intervention', *Rehabilitation Psychology* 38(1), pp. 3–10.

Brock, Brian (2019), *Wondrously Wounded: Theology, Disability and the Body of Christ*, Waco, TX: Baylor University Press.

Brown, Judith (2016), 'Recurrent grief in mothering a child with an intellectual disability to adulthood: grieving is the healing', *Child and Family Social Work*, 21(1), pp. 113–22.

Brown, Stephanie et al. (1994), *Missing Voices: The Experience of Motherhood*, Melbourne: Oxford University Press.

Burack, Jacob A. et al. (2001), *The Development of Autism: Perspectives from Theory and Research*, London: Erlbaum.

Bury, Mike (2010), 'Chronic illness, self-management and the rhetoric of empowerment', in G. Scambler and S. Scambler (eds), *New Directions in the Sociology of Chronic and Disabling Conditions: Assaults on the Lifeworld*, Basingstoke: Palgrave Macmillan.

Butler, Judith (1999), *Gender Trouble*, New York: Routledge.

Butz, David and K. Besio (2009), 'Autoethnography', *Geography Compass*, 3(5), pp. 1660–74.

Campbell, Jane and Mike Oliver (1996), *Disability Politics: Understanding Our Past, Changing Our Future*, London: Routledge.

Cerbone, David (2006), *Understanding Phenomenology*, London: Routledge.

Claiborne Park, Clara (1995), *The Siege: A Family's Journey into the World of an Autistic Child*, Boston, MA: Little, Brown Book Group, reprint of 1967 edn.

Claiborne Park, Clara (2002), *Exiting Nirvana: A Daughter's Life with Autism*, London: Little, Brown Book Group.

Clarke, T. et al. (2016), 'Common polygenic risk for autism spectrum disorder (ASD) is associated with cognitive ability in the general population', *Molecular Psychiatry*, 21(3), pp. 419–25.

Creamer, Deborah (2009), *Disability and Christian Theology: Embodied Limits and Constructive Possibilities*, New York: Oxford University Press.

Creamer, Deborah (2012), 'Disability theology', *Religion Compass*, 6(7), pp. 339–46.

Cross, Katie (2020), *The Sunday Assembly and Theologies of Suffer-

ing (Explorations in Practical, Pastoral, and Empirical Theology), London: Routledge.

Crow, Liz (1996), 'Including all of our lives: renewing the social model of disability', available from www.roaring-girl.com/wp-content/uploads/2013/07/Including-All-of-Our-Lives.pdf, accessed 20.05.21.

Daly, Mary (1986), *Beyond God the Father: Toward a Philosophy of Women's Liberation*, London: The Women's Press.

Davis, Lennard (2013), *The End of Normal: Identity in a Biocultural Era*, Ann Arbor, MI: University of Michigan Press.

De Certeau, Michel (1988), *The Practice of Everyday Life*, trans. by Steven Rendall, Berkeley, CA and London: University of California Press.

Denzin, Norman (2003), *Performance Ethnography: Critical Pedagogy and the Politics of Culture*, Thousand Oaks, CA and London: Sage Publications.

Dowling, Monica and Linda Dolan (2001), 'Families with children with disabilities: inequalities and the social model', *Disability and Society*, 16, pp. 21–35.

DuBose, T. (1997), 'The phenomenology of bereavement, grief and mourning', *Journal of Religion and Health*, 36, pp. 367–74.

Duerte, Cristiane et al. (2005), 'Factors associated with stress in mothers of children with autism', *Autism*, 9(4), pp. 416–27.

Durant, W. (1946), 'What is civilization?', *Ladies Home Journal*, 23 (January), p. 107.

Eakes, Georgene (1995), 'Chronic sorrow: the lived experience of parents of chronically mentally ill individuals', *Psychiatric Nursing*, April, 9(2), pp. 77–84.

Eiesland, Nancy (1994), *The Disabled God: Toward a Liberatory Theology of Disability*, Nashville, TN: Abingdon Press.

Ellis, Carolyn and Arthur Bochner (2003), 'Autoethnography, personal narrative, reflexivity: researcher as subject', in N. Denzin and Y. Lincoln (eds), *Collecting and Interpreting Qualitative Materials*, 2nd edn, pp. 199–258.

Estes, Annette et al. (2009), 'Parenting stress and psychological functioning among mothers of preschool children with autism and developmental delay', *Autism*, 13(4), pp. 375–87.

Evans, Bonnie (2013), 'How autism became autism: the radical transformation of a central concept of child development in Britain', *History of the Human Sciences*, 26(3), pp. 3–31.

Fernandez, Manuel et al. (2016), 'Feelings of loss and grief in parents of children diagnosed with Autism Spectrum Disorder (ASD)', *Research in Developmental Disabilities*, 55, pp. 312–21.

Foucault, Michel (1978), *The History of Sexuality Vol. 1: An Introduction*, trans. by Robert Hurley, New York: Random House.

Frith, Uta (ed.) (1991), *Autism and Asperger Syndrome*, Cambridge: Cambridge University Press.

Frith, Uta (2003), *Autism: Explaining the Enigma*, Oxford: Blackwell Publishing.

Gabriels, Robin and Dina Hill (2002), *Autism – From Research to Individualized Practice*, London: Jessica Kingsley Publishers.

Ganzevoort, R. Ruard (2012), 'Narrative approaches', in B. Miller-McLemore, *The Wiley-Blackwell Companion to Practical Theology*, Oxford: Blackwell Publishing, pp. 214–23.

Garland-Thomson, Rosemarie (2011), 'Integrating disability: transforming feminist theory', in K. Hall (ed.), *Feminist Disability Studies*, Bloomington, IN: Indiana University Press, pp. 13–47.

Geiger, Susan (1986), 'Women's life histories: method and content', *Signs* 11(2), pp. 334–51.

Giallo, Rebecca et al. (2013), 'Fatigue, wellbeing and parental self-efficacy in mothers of children with an Autism Spectrum Disorder', *Autism*, 17(4), pp. 465–80.

Gill, J. and P. Liamputtong (2011), 'Being the mother of a child with Asperger's Syndrome: women's experiences of stigma', *Health Care for Women International*, 32(8), pp. 708–22.

Gillibrand, J. (2010), *Disabled Church – Disabled Society: The Implications of Autism for Philosophy, Theology and Politics*, London: Jessica Kingsley Publishers.

Goffman, Erving (1990), *Stigma: Notes on the Management of Spoiled Identity*, London: Penguin, reprint of 1963 edition.

Goto, Courtney (2018), *Taking on Practical Theology: The Idolization of Context and the Hope of Community*, Leiden: Brill.

Graham, Elaine (1995), *Making the Difference: Gender, Personhood and Theology*, London: Mowbray.

Graham, Elaine (1996), *Transforming Practice: Pastoral Theology in an Age of Uncertainty*, London: Mowbray.

Graham, Elaine (2013), *Between a Rock and a Hard place: Public Theology in a Post-Secular Age*, London: SCM Press.

Graham, Elaine, Heather Walton and Francis Ward (2018), *Theological Reflection: Methods Volume 2*, London: SCM Press.

Grandin, Temple (1996), *Emergence: Labeled Autistic*, New York: Warner Books.

Gray, David (1993), 'Perceptions of stigma: the parents of autistic children', *Sociology of Health & Illness*, 15(1), pp. 102–20.

Gray, David (1997), 'High functioning autistic children and the construction of "normal family life"', *Social Science & Medicine*, 44(8), pp. 1097–106.

Green, S. E. (2007), '"We're tired, not sad": benefits and burdens of mothering a child with a disability', *Social Science & Medicine*, 64(1), pp. 150–63.

Gutiérrez, Gustavo (1973), *A Theology of Liberation*, Maryknoll: NY, Orbis Books.

Hacking, Ian (2009), 'Autistic autobiography', *Philosophical Transactions of the Royal Society B*, 364(1522), pp. 1467–73.

Hall, Kim (2011), *Feminist Disability Studies*, Bloomington, IN: Indiana University Press.

Haraway, D. (1988), 'Situated knowledges: the science question in feminism and the privilege of partial perspective', *Feminist Studies*, 14(3), pp. 575–99.

Harding, Sandra (2007), *Whose Science? Whose Knowledge? Thinking from Women's Lives*, Milton Keynes: Open University Press.

Harris, Darcy (2019), *Non-death Loss and Grief: Context and Clinical Implications*, London: Routledge.

Hauerwas, Stanley (1990), *Naming the Silences: God, Medicine and the Problem of Suffering*, London: T&T Clark International.

Hauerwas, Stanley (2005), 'The Church and the mentally handicapped', *Journal of Religion, Disability & Health*, 8(3–4), pp. 53–62.

Healey, Nicholas (2014), *Hauerwas: A (Very) Critical Introduction (Interventions)*, Grand Rapids, MI: Wm B. Erdmans Publishing.

Heidegger, Martin (1996), *Being and Time: A Second Translation of Sein und Zeit*, trans. by Joan Stambaugh, New York: State University of New York Press, reprint of 1953 edn.

Hoffman, Charles et al. (2009), 'Parenting stress and closeness: mothers of typically developing children and mothers of children with autism', *Focus on Autism and Other Disabilities*, 24(3), pp. 178–9.

Holman-Jones, Stacey (2005), 'Autoethnography: making the personal political', in N. Denzin and Y. Lincoln , *Sage Handbook of Qualitative Research*, 3rd edn, Thousand Oaks, CA: Sage Publications, pp. 763–92.

Holton, Avery et al. (2012), 'The blame frame: media attribution of culpability about the MMR–autism vaccination scare', *Health Communication*, 27(7), pp. 690–701.

Howell, Paul (2015), 'From *Rain Man* to *Sherlock*: theological reflections on metaphor and ASD', *Practical Theology*, 8(2), pp. 143–53.

Howlin, Patricia (1996), *Autism: Preparing for Adulthood*, London: Routledge.

Howlin, Patricia and A. Asgharian (1999), 'The diagnosis of autism and Asperger syndrome: findings from a survey of 770 families', *Developmental Medicine and Child Neurology*, 41(12), pp. 834–39.

Hughes, Bill, D. Goodley and L. Davis (2012), *Disability and Social Theory: New Developments and Directions*, London: Palgrave Macmillan.

Hull, John M. (2001), *In the Beginning There Was Darkness: A Blind Person's Conversations with the Bible*, London: SCM Press.

Husserl, Edmund (1970), *Logical Investigations* (2 vols), trans. by J. N Findlay, London: Routledge.

IBCCES, 'Interview with Dr Stephen Shore: Autism Advocate and on the Spectrum', *IBCCES*, https://ibcces.org/blog/2018/03/23/12748/, accessed 12.03.19.

International Classification of Diseases (2016), 'International Classification of Diseases', https://icd.who.int/browse10/2016/en#/F84.5, accessed 12.03.19.

Isasi-Díaz, Ada María (1996), *Mujerista Theology: A Theology for the Twenty-First Century*, Maryknoll, NY: Orbis Books.

Isasi-Díaz, Ada María (2004), *En La Lucha – In the Struggle: Elaborating a Mujerista Theology*, Minneapolis, MN: Fortress Press.

Isasi-Díaz, Ada María (2011), 'Mujerista discourse: a platform for Latinas' subjugated knowledge', in A. M. Isasi-Díaz and E. Mendieta, *Decolonizing Epistemologies: Latina/o Theology and Philosophy*, New York: Fordham University Press, pp. 44–67.

Kanner, Leo (1943), 'Autistic disturbances of affective contact', *Nervous Child*, 2, pp. 217–50.

Kanner, Leo (1949), 'Problems of nosology and psychodynamics of early infantile autism', *American Journal of Orthopsychiatry*, 19(3), pp. 416–26.

Kanner, Leo (1958), 'The specificity of early infantile autism', *Kinderpsychiatrie*, 25(1), pp.108–13.

Kearney, P. and T. Griffin (2006), 'Between joy and sorrow: being a parent of a child with a developmental disability', *Journal of Advanced Nursing*, 34(5), pp. 582–92.

Kelly, Melissa (2010), *Grief: Contemporary Theory and the Practice of Ministry*, Minneapolis, MN: Fortress Press.

Kenny, Lorcan et al. (2016), 'Which terms should be used to describe autism? Perspectives from the UK autism community', *Autism*, 20(4), pp. 442–62.

King, G. A. et al. (2006), 'A qualitative investigation of changes in the belief systems of families of children with autism or Down syndrome', *Child: Care, Health and Development*, 32(3), pp. 353–69.

Knickmeyer, Rebecca and S. Baron-Cohen (2006), 'Foetal development and sex differences in typical social development and in autism', *Journal of Child Neurology*, 21(10), pp. 825–45.

Kocabiyik, Oya and Y. Fazlioglu (2018), 'Life stories of parents with autistic children', *Journal of Education and Training Studies*, 6(3), pp. 26–37.

Koenig, K., C. Tstanis and F. Volkmar (2001), 'Neurobiology and genetics of autism: a developmental perspective', in J. A. Burack et al. (eds), *The Development of Autism: Perspectives from Theory and Research*, London: Erlbaum, pp. 81–104.

Kübler-Ross, Elisabeth (1997), *On Death and Dying*, London: Routledge.

Kwok, Pui-lan (2011), 'The politics and poetics of Ada María Isasi-Díaz', *Feminist Theology*, 20(1), pp. 33–8.

Laird, Joan (1991), 'Women and stories: restorying women's self-constructions' in M. McGoldrick, C. M. Anderson and F. Walsh (eds), *Women and Families: A Framework for Family Therapy*, New York: W. W. Norton & Co.

Lawson, Wendy (2008), *Concepts of Normality: The Autistic and Typical Spectrum*, London: Jessica Kingsley Publishers.

Lecavalier, L. (2006), 'Behavioral and emotional problems in young people with pervasive developmental disorders: relative prevalence, effects of subject characteristics, and empirical classification', *Journal of Autism and Developmental Disorders*, 36(8), pp. 1101–14.

Lexhed, Jenny (2015), *Love Is Not Enough: A Mother's Memoir of Autism, Madness and Hope*, New York: Arcade Publishing.

Loveland, K. A. (2001), 'Toward an ecological theory of autism', in J. A. Burack et al. (eds), *The Development of Autism: Perspectives from Theory and Research*, Mahwah, NJ: Erlbaum.

Macaskill, Grant (2019), *Autism and the Church: Bible, Theology and Community*, Waco, TX: Baylor University Press.

MacKay et al. (2018), 'The microsegmentation of the autism spectrum: a research project', available from www.gov.scot/publications/microsegmentation-autism-spectrum/pages/9/, accessed 12.02.20.

Mathew, Stephen K. and J. D. Pandian (2010), 'Newer insights to the neurological diseases among biblical characters of old testament', *Annals of Indian Academy of Neurology*, 13(3), pp. 164–6.

Mayes, Susan et al. (2012), 'Autism and ADHD: overlapping and discriminating symptoms', *Research in Autism Spectrum Disorders*, 6(1), pp. 277–85.

Mazzei, Lisa A. and Alecia Y. Jackson (2012), 'Complicating voice in a refusal to "let participants speak for themselves"', *Qualitative Inquiry*, 18(9), pp. 745–51.

McGuire, Anne (2016), *War on Autism: On the Cultural Logic of Normative Violence*, Ann Arbor, MI: University of Michigan Press.

Merleau-Ponty, M. (1962), *Phenomenology of Perception*, trans. by C. Smith, London: Routledge.

Miller-McLemore, Bonnie J. (1994), *Also a Mother: Work and Family as Theological Drama*, Nashville, TN: Abingdon Press.

Miller-McLemore, Bonnie J. (2012), *The Wiley-Blackwell Companion to Practical Theology*, Oxford: Blackwell Publishing.

Miller-McLemore, Bonnie and J. Mercer (2016), *Conundrums in Practical Theology*, Leiden: Brill.

Morris, Jenny (1992), 'Personal and political: a feminist perspective on researching physical disability', *Disability, Handicap & Society*, 7(2), pp. 157–66.

Morris, Jenny (1996), *Encounters with Strangers: Feminism and Disability*, London: The Women's Press.

Moschella, Mary Clark (2016), *Caring for Joy: Narrative, Theology and Practice*, Leiden: Brill.

Nicholas, David B. et al. (2016), '"Live it to understand it": the experiences of mothers of children with autism spectrum disorder', *Qualitative Health Research*, 26(7), pp. 921–34.

Nouwen, Henri (1997), *Adam: God's Beloved*, New York: Orbis Books.

Odland, Sarah (2010), 'Unassailable motherhood, ambivalent domesticity: The construction of maternal identity in the Ladies Home Journal in 1946', *Journal of Communication Inquiry*, 34(1), pp. 61–84.

Olassen, Virginia (2005), 'Early millenial feminist qualitative research: challenges and contours', in N. Denzin and Y. Lincoln, *Sage Handbook of Qualitative Research*, 3rd edn, Thousand Oaks, CA: Sage Publications, pp. 235–78.

Oliver, Michael (1990) *The Politics of Disablement*, London: Palgrave Macmillan.

Parsons, Talcott (1951), *The Social System*, London: Free Press of Glencoe.

Prout, A. and C. Hallett (2003), *Hearing the Voices of Children: Social Policy for a New Century*, London: RoutledgeFalmer.

Rambo, Shelly (2010), *Spirit and Trauma: A Theology of Remaining*, Louisville, KY: Westminster John Knox.

Randles, Clint (2012), 'Phenomenology, a review of the literature', *Update: Applications of Research in Music Education*, 30(2), pp. 11–21.

Reynolds, Tom (2008), *Vulnerable Communion: A Theology of Disability and Hospitality*, Grand Rapids, MI: Brazos Press.

Rich, Adrienne (1996), *Of Woman Born: Motherhood as Experience and Institution* (reprint), London: W.W. Norton & Co.

Ricoeur, Paul (1991), *A Ricoeur Reader: Reflection and Imagination*, Toronto: University of Toronto Press.

Rilke, Rainer Maria (1921), 'Duino Elegies', trans. by E. Sackville-West and V. Sackville-West (1931), in *Duineser Elegien: Elegies from the Castle of Duino*, London: The Hogarth Press.

Rimland, Bernard (1964), *Infantile Autism: The Syndrome and Its Implications for a Neural Theory of Behaviour*, London: Methuen.

Robinson, Oliver (2014), 'Sampling in interview-based qualitative research: a theoretical and practical guide', *Qualitative Research in Psychology*, 11(1), pp. 25–41.

Ruddick, Sara (1990), *Maternal Thinking: Towards a Politics of Peace*, London: The Women's Press.

Runswick-Cole, Katherine and Rebecca Mallett (2014), *Approaching Disability: Critical Issues and Perspectives*, London: Routledge.

Rutter, Michael (1970), 'Autistic children: infancy to adulthood', *Seminars in Psychiatry*, 2(4), pp. 435–50.

Samuels, Ellen (2011), 'Critical divides: Judith Butler's body theory and the question of disability', in K. Hall (ed.), *Feminist Disability Studies*, Bloomington, IN: Indiana University Press, pp. 48–66.

Sansosti, Frank J., K. B. Lavik and J. M. Sansosti (2012), 'Family experiences through the autism diagnostic process', *Focus on Autism and Other Developmental Difficulties*, 27(2), pp. 81–90.

Schaff, Roseann et al. (2011), 'The everyday routines of families of children with autism: examining the impact of sensory processing difficulties on the family', *Autism*, 15(3), pp. 373–89.

Schulman, Cory (2002), 'Bridging the process between diagnosis and treatment', in R. Gabriels and D. Hill (2002), *Autism – From Research to Individualized Practice*, London: Jessica Kingsley Publishers, pp. 25–46.

Schüssler Fiorenza, Elisabeth (1996), *The Power of Naming: A Concilium Reader in Feminist Liberation Theology*, London: SCM Press.

Scottish Commission for Learning Disabilities, 'The Keys to Life', Scottish Commission for People with Learning Difficulties, www.scld.org.uk/the-keys-to-life/, accessed 03.09.19.

Shakespeare, Tom and Nick Watson (2010), 'Beyond models: understanding the complexity of disabled people's lives', in G. Scambler and S. Scambler (eds), *New Directions in the Sociology of Chronic and Disabling Conditions: Assaults on the Lifeworld*, Basingstoke: Palgrave Macmillan.

Shore, Stephen and Linda Rastelli (2006), *Understanding Autism for Dummies*, Hoboken, NJ: Wiley.

Silberman, Steve (2015), *Neurotribes: The Legacy of Autism and How to Think Smarter About People Who Think Differently*, New York: Allen and Unwin.

Simonoff, E. et al. (2008), 'Psychiatric disorders in children with autism spectrum disorders: prevalence, comorbidity, and associated factors in a population derived sample', *Journal of American Child Adolescent Psychiatry*, 47(8), pp. 921–9.

Slee, Nicola (2017), 'A spirituality for multiple overwhelmings', *Practical Theology*, 10(1), pp. 20–32.

Smith, Brett and A. Sparkes (2008), 'Contrasting perspectives on narrating selves and identities: an invitation to dialogue', *Qualitative Research*, 8(1), pp. 5–35.

Sotirin, Patty (2010), 'Autoethnographic mother-writing: advocating radical specificity', *Journal of Research Practice*, 6(1), pp. 1–15.

Spiker, Michael et al. (2012), 'Restricted interests and anxiety in children with autism', *Autism*, 16(3), pp. 306–20.

Spry, Tami (2011), *Body, Paper, Stage: Writing and Performing Auto-ethnography*, Walnut Creek, CA: Left Coast Press.

Stephenson, J. S. and D. Murphy (1986), 'Existential grief: the special case of the chronically ill and disabled', *Death Studies*, 10(2), pp. 135–45.

Stewart, Mary et al. (2006), 'Presentation of depression in autism and Asperger syndrome', *Autism*, 10(1), pp. 103–16.

Stillman, William (2006), *Autism and the God Connection: Redefining the Autistic Experience Through Extraordinary Accounts of Spiritual Giftedness*, Naperville, IL: Sourcebooks.

Streck, Valburga Schmiedt (2012), 'Brazil', in B. Miller-McLemore (ed.), *The Wiley-Blackwell Companion to Practical Theology*, Oxford: Blackwell Publishing, pp. 534–43.

Stroebe, Margaret and Henk Schut (1999), 'The dual process model of coping with bereavement: rationale and description', *Death Studies*, 23(3), pp. 197–224.

Swinton, John (1997), 'Friendship in community: creating a space for love', *Contact*, 122(1), pp. 17–22.

Swinton, John (2003), 'The body of Christ has Down's Syndrome: theological reflections on vulnerability, disability, and graceful communities', *Journal of Pastoral Theology*, 13(2), pp. 66–78.

Swinton, John and Stanley Hauerwas (2005), *Critical Reflections on Stanley Hauerwas' Theology of Disability: Disabling Society, Enabling Theology*, New York: Haworth Press.

Swinton, John and Harriet Mowat (2006), *Practical Theology and Qualitative Research*, London: SCM Press.

Swinton, John and Christine Trevett (2009), 'Religion and autism: initiating an interdisciplinary conversation', *Journal of Religion, Disability and Health*, 12(1), pp. 2–6.

Swinton, John (2012a), 'Disability, ableism and disablism', in B. Miller-McLemore (ed.), *The Wiley-Blackwell Companion to Practical Theology*, Oxford: Blackwell Publishing, pp. 443–51.

Swinton, John (2012b), 'Reflections on autistic love: what does love look like?', *Practical Theology*, 5(3), pp. 259–78.

Swinton, John (2012c), 'From inclusion to belonging: a practical theology of community, disability and humanness', *Journal of Religion, Disability and Health*, 16(2), pp. 172–90.

Swinton, J. (2012d), *Dementia: Living in the Memories of God*, London: SCM Press.

Tager-Flusberg, Helen (2001), 'A re-examination of the theory of mind hypothesis of autism', in J. Burack et al., *The Development of Autism: Perspectives from Theory and Research*, Mahwah, NJ: Erlbaum, pp. 173–93.

Thomas, Carol (2002), 'Disability theory: key ideas, issues and thinkers', in C. Barnes, M. Oliver and L. Barton, *Disability Studies Today*, Cambridge: Polity Press.

Thomas, Carol (2010), 'Medical sociology and disability theory' in G. Scambler and S. Scambler, *New Directions in the Sociology of Chronic and Disabling Conditions: Assaults on the Lifeworld*, Basingstoke: Palgrave Macmillan.

Tomeney, Theodore (2017), 'Parenting stress as an indirect pathway to mental health concerns among mothers of children with autism spectrum disorder autism', *Autism*, 21(7), pp. 907–91.

Tsatsanis, Katherine D. and F. R. Volkmar (2001), 'Neurobiology and genetics of autism: a developmental perspective', in J. A. Burack et al (eds), *The Development of Autism: Perspectives from Theory and Research*', Mahwah, NJ: Erlbaum.

Van der Ven, Johannes (1993), *Practical Theology: An Empirical Approach*, Kampen, Netherlands: Kok Pharos Publishing House.

Veling, Terry (2005), *Practical Theology: On Earth as it is in Heaven*, New York: Orbis Books.

Waiting for Assessment Executive Summary (2014), ACHIEVE Alliance, www.autismnetworkscotland.org.uk/files/2014/11/AAA-ASD-Waiting-for-Assessment-Executive-Summary.pdf, accessed 12.02.20.

Wakefield, Andrew (1999), 'MMR vaccine and autism', *The Lancet*, 354(9182), pp. 949–50.

Walton, Heather (2001), 'The wisdom of Sheba: constructing feminist practical theology', *Contact*, 135(1), pp. 3–12.

Walton, Heather (2014a), 'Seeking wisdom in Practical Theology', *Practical Theology*, 7(1), pp. 5–18.

Walton, Heather (2014b), *Writing Methods in Theological Reflection*, London: SCM Press.

Walton, Heather (2018), 'We have never been theologians: post-secularism and practical theology', *Practical Theology*, 11(3), pp. 218–30.

Walton, Heather (2020), 'Life writing', unpublished article.

Waltz, Mitzi (2013), *Autism: A Social and Medical History*, Basingstoke: Palgrave Macmillan.

Watson, Nick (2007), *Disability: Major Themes in Health and Social Welfare*, London: Routledge.

Wendell, Susan (1997), *The Rejected Body: Feminist Philosophical Reflections on Disability*, London: Routledge.

Whittingham, K. et al. (2013), 'Predictors of psychological adjustment, experienced parenting burden and chronic sorrow symptoms in parents of children with cerebral palsy', *Child: Care, Health and Development*, 39(3), pp. 366–73.

Wing, Lorna (1996), *The Autistic Spectrum: A Guide for Parents and Professionals*, London: Constable.

Wolfteich, Claire (2017), *Mothering, Public Leadership and Women's*

Life Writing: Explorations in Spirituality Studies and Practical Theology, Leiden: Brill.

Zelazo, Philip A. (2001), 'Developmental perspective on early autism: affective, behavioural, and cognitive factors', in J. A. Burack et al. (eds), *The Development of Autism: Perspectives from Theory and Research*, London: Erlbaum, pp. 39–60.

Zhang, Wei et al. (2015), 'Post-traumatic growth in mothers of children with autism: a phenomenological study', *Autism*, 19(1), pp. 29–37.

Index of Names and Subjects